A Culinary History of
MOBILE

A Culinary History of MOBILE

CHRIS ANDREWS

AMERICAN PALATE

Published by American Palate
A Division of The History Press
Charleston, SC
www.historypress.com

Copyright © 2023 by Christopher Andrews
All rights reserved

First published 2023

Manufactured in the United States

ISBN 9781467149051

Library of Congress Control Number: 2023938567

Notice: The information in this book is true and complete to the best of our knowledge. It is offered without guarantee on the part of the author or The History Press. The author and The History Press disclaim all liability in connection with the use of this book.

All rights reserved. No part of this book may be reproduced or transmitted in any form whatsoever without prior written permission from the publisher except in the case of brief quotations embodied in critical articles and reviews.

This book is dedicated to my children: Audrey, Sawyer and Carson.

Audrey thinks I am writing a book about bananas, Sawyer wonders if this is a "real book" and Carson said he is going to write a book someday.

I love you and couldn't be prouder to be your dad!

Contents

Acknowledgements 9
Introduction 13

Part I. Foundations of Flavor: The Roots of Mobile's Culinary Heritage
1. Pearls of the Past: Oysters, Native Americans and
    Wintzell's Oyster House 17
2. Inking the Past: The Founding of Mobile and Squid Ink 24
3. Stirring the Pot of History: The Royal Scam's Gumbo
    and Colonial Mobile 35

Part II. Harvest and Hardship: The Intersection of History
 and Food in Mobile's Nineteenth Century
4. From Oyster Saloons to Oakleigh: Callaghan's Irish Social Club
    and the Culinary Landscape of Mobile in the 1800s 45
5. From Chains to Freedom: The Story of Kazoola and
    Early African American Foodways 53
6. Cracking the Shell: The A&M Peanut Shop and
    Civil War Legacies in Mobile 62

Part III. The Melting Pot: Immigrant Influences and Culinary
 Progress in Twentieth-Century Mobile
7. The Changing Table: The Dew Drop Inn and the
    Culinary Scene of Mobile in the 1900s 73

Contents

8. A Sweet Legacy: Greek Immigrants and the Legacy
    of Three Georges 86
9. From Havana to Mobile: Prohibition Tales and
    Cuban Connections at Las Floriditas 93

PART IV. A NEW ERA OF EATS: MOBILE'S TWENTY-FIRST-CENTURY
    FOOD REVOLUTION
10. Carnival Cuisine: King Cakes, Moon Pies and
    the Joe Cain Cafe.. 105
11. Home Runs, Huddles and Hometown Favorites:
    A Journey Through Mobile's Sports History at
    Heroes Sports Bar and Grille 116
12. From Revitalization to Revolution: The Cheese Cottage
    and Mobile's Twenty-First-Century Food Scene 123

Conclusion 133
Bibliography.. 135
About the Author 141

ACKNOWLEDGEMENTS

I first want to thank my wife, Laney. She not only puts up with me and my crazy adventures on a daily basis but has been incredibly supportive of this book project as well. When Laney and I first started Bienville Bites Food Tour in 2017, she was right there every step of the way. She and I gave every tour for the first year and a half of our food tour venture. With this book project, she was in my corner again. There were a lot of late nights and a lot of books scattered all over her living room, and she bore the brunt of a lot of my frustration throughout this project. Thank you, Laney!

The idea of writing this book first came to me amid the COVID-19 pandemic when I found myself contacting The History Press. The world was in lockdown, and Bienville Bites Food Tour was temporarily shuttered with no clear reopening date in sight. My personal life, once filled with hours on the T-ball and soccer fields, had come to an abrupt halt, leaving me with an unusual abundance of spare time. What better use of this time, I thought, than to write a book? With a wealth of research and countless food tours under my belt, not to mention the countless stories about Mobile's history and food that I had shared, it seemed like a straightforward task.

Having said that, I am forever indebted to Joe Gartrell of The History Press. I recall our initial conversation when I naively promised to have the book ready in a matter of months. I'm deeply grateful for his patience. A few weeks after I submitted the idea for this book to The History Press, the

Acknowledgements

world did reopen, at least it did in South Alabama. Our food tours had slowly begun to reopen, and then Laney and I had the craziest idea of anyone in the world, literally. We started a food tour in Fairhope, Alabama, in November 2020. Taste of Fairhope was the only food tour in the world that started in 2020 post-pandemic. We had no idea what was about to happen in the restaurant industry in 2021 with staffing shortages, rising food costs and the incredible demand from the community to eat at locally owned restaurants. Despite these challenges, our tours have continued to grow, and my book project kept getting delayed. Thank you for hanging with me and helping me, Joe!

I want to thank my colleagues and fellow tour guides at Bienville Bites Food Tour: Dannette, Katherine, Isabella and Lee. They consistently give five-star-rated tours, and their hard work and dedication to our mission of connecting people to the city of Mobile does not go unnoticed for one second. Similarly, I also want to thank our team of tour guides at Taste of Fairhope: Parker, Savannah and Jennifer have delivered unforgettable experiences each and every week to our guests in Fairhope. I couldn't be more excited about the future of our tours in Mobile and Fairhope with this excellent team!

As I look back on the journey of crafting this book, I am awestruck by the depth and richness of Mobile's culinary history. From the city's earliest days to the culinary renaissance of today, Mobile's food scene has always been a melting pot of cultures, traditions and flavors. However, it is important to remember that this book is merely a snapshot, a taste of the city's vibrant and ever-evolving food scene. While the stories within these pages highlight some of Mobile's most iconic and influential establishments, they represent only a fraction of the city's rich culinary tapestry. There are countless other eateries, past and present, each with its own unique story, that add to the flavor of our city. To the restaurants and chefs not featured in this volume, know that your contributions to Mobile's culinary landscape are no less significant. Each eatery, from the food truck down the street to the most sophisticated fine-dining establishment, adds a unique page to Mobile's culinary success. Each chef, from the line cook to the James Beard Award nominees, plays a vital role in our city's food scene.

This book is not meant to be an exhaustive record of Mobile's culinary history but rather a tribute to the city's food culture. It is a celebration of the diversity, creativity and resilience that have shaped Mobile's food scene and a testament to the city's enduring love for good food. Perhaps, one day, there will be another book that delves deeper into the untold stories of Mobile's culinary history. There are certainly more tales to tell, more dishes to sample and more milestones to celebrate. But for now, I hope this book whets your appetite and leaves you hungry for more.

Finally, I want to extend my deepest gratitude to everyone who has been a part of this journey. To the restaurateurs, chefs and historians who graciously shared their stories and their passion for food, thank you. To the readers, thank you for joining me on this culinary adventure. Here's to many more delicious chapters in Mobile's culinary story.

INTRODUCTION

Mobile, Alabama: a city that evokes the warmth of southern hospitality, a destination that exudes the charm of centuries-old architecture, a place where the vibrant pulse of the present is perfectly harmonized with the echoes of the past. This is a city where the Spanish moss–draped oaks stand as grand sentinels, each whispering the tales of time. It's where the mighty Mobile River flows like a life vein, carrying centuries of stories from all over the world to the bustling port, making this city a convergence of cultures, histories and flavor.

Mobile's culinary scene, as diverse and dynamic as its people, is a reflection of its storied past and promising future. Each restaurant, each dish, each recipe is a testament to the city's resilience, innovation and enduring love for great food. From the first inhabitants who drew sustenance from the land and sea to the waves of immigrants bringing their unique culinary traditions and finally to the modern-day culinary renaissance of today, culinary artists and entrepreneurs are continually reinventing the city's food scene. Mobile's food history is as rich as the gumbo that simmers in its kitchens.

Mobile sits at an interesting corner of the globe, where the flavors of the South mingle with the influences of Europe, Africa and the Caribbean. Its geographic location—where the Mobile River dumps into Mobile Bay, which conversely empties into the Gulf of Mexico—has given it access to a bounty of fresh seafood, while its soil is just fertile enough to yield crops that have been staples of southern cooking for generations. But

Introduction

the culinary story of Mobile is not just about the food itself; it's about the people who have prepared and served it and the cultural exchanges that have happened around the dining table. From the Native Americans to the French, Spanish and British colonizers, African slaves and waves of immigrants, each group has contributed to the city's unique culinary tapestry. And it's a history that extends beyond the borders of downtown, to the burgeoning food scenes in surrounding neighborhoods of the Oakleigh Garden District, Midtown, West Mobile and beyond.

In this book, you will learn about not only the origins of Mobile's iconic dishes but also the stories of the people and places behind them. As you turn these pages, you'll also discover the innovative spirit that propels Mobile's food scene near the top of the list as a dining destination in the South. You will visit iconic eateries, from long-standing institutions like Wintzell's Oyster House and the Dew Drop Inn to the innovative establishments redefining the city's food scene today.

Through the chapters of this book, I invite you to share in the delicious legacy of Mobile. This isn't just a book about food; it's a celebration of a city's history, its people and the shared experiences that connect us all. Whether you are a longtime resident of Mobile or a newcomer, I hope this book will ignite a sense of pride and excitement for our city's culinary journey, and may it inspire you to explore and taste the incredible food culture that Mobile offers. So, grab a seat, and let's dig into the culinary history of Mobile.

My hope is that you will not just read about Mobile's food history, but you will feel, smell and taste it. Just like the mission for each and every one of our food tours at Bienville Bites Food Tour, my goal is to connect you to the city of Mobile and give you an experience that will last a lifetime. Let's go!

PART I
FOUNDATIONS OF FLAVOR

THE ROOTS OF MOBILE'S CULINARY HERITAGE

1
PEARLS OF THE PAST

OYSTERS, NATIVE AMERICANS AND WINTZELL'S OYSTER HOUSE

Welcome to Wintzell's! The man who parked your car doesn't work here.

Upon arrival at the iconic Wintzell's Oyster House, Mobile's oldest oyster bar, located along historic Dauphin Street, you will quickly find hundreds of hand-painted sayings adorning the walls. These are the creation of the quick-witted J. Oliver Wintzell. "Customers used to ask me a lot of questions," Wintzell once said to a journalist. "It was hard to answer them and get the oysters opened, so I started the signs to get across some of the information they wanted. Now they keep so busy reading, they don't ask questions."

In 1938, J. Oliver Wintzell opened his six-stool oyster bar serving only raw oysters. Despite the country being in the middle of the Great Depression, he found out one thing: Mobilians are crazy about oysters! It may have been the fact that oysters were fifteen cents per dozen in those days. It could also be that Oliver Wintzell's rent at the iconic location on Dauphin Street was originally eight dollars per month, not counting his first four months, which were free, or it could just be the fact that as Mobilians, it is our birthright to enjoy oysters. No matter your economic status, oysters are what we eat, and at Wintzell's Oyster House they are famously served "fried, stewed and nude." Shortly after opening his business, Wintzell purchased his own 190-acre oyster reef farm at Portersville Bay, twenty miles south of Mobile. Portersville Bay was said to have produced the finest oysters in the country by scientists of the U.S. Bureau of Fisheries and by J. Oliver Wintzell himself.

Word quickly spread around the Southeast about Wintzell's Oyster House, a landmark restaurant in Mobile even to this day.

Mobile, Alabama, has been referred to as "The Big Oyster," and why not? It's a significant part of our culture. Oysters are fundamental to who we are. Oysters bring jobs to our area for the hardworking people who harvest them. Distributers ship them to our local restaurants where men and women serve them daily in our local seafood restaurants. Oysters provide satisfaction to hungry patrons looking to enjoy a good meal. Four-foot fiberglass oysters are spread throughout town in parks, restaurants and lobbies. Each of these oysters has been painted by local artists and includes information about how oysters benefit Mobile Bay and the surrounding area. Oysters are the signature dish of Mobile.

The story of oysters in Mobile can be traced back long before J. Oliver Wintzell shucked the first oyster at his Dauphin Street location in 1938 and long before the Europeans arrived and permanently settled Fort Louis de la Mobile in 1702. People have been living on our shores for thousands of years. People have built communities, explored, fought and eaten on the same shores that we live today. Mobile's story begins in a time that archaeologists refer to as the Woodland period. Three archaeological explorations have been uncovered along the Mobile River that date to this period. Woodland people lived as hunters and gatherers. The use of bow and arrow, a technological marvel at the time, allowed the men to kill animals. Deer, bear, buffalo, turtle and wild turkey were hunted, cleaned and cooked over a small fire before being eaten. Fish, oysters and clams were caught, harvested and consumed. They gathered nuts and berries to store. They kept regular gardens and cultivated plants, beans and grains, something their ancestors did not. This greatly improved the variety and reliability of their food supply. With this abundance of food supply came a need for pottery to store the food. Jars made of sand, limestone and clay were used.

The centuries between AD 1000 and 1500 are commonly known as the Mississippian period, a time that preceded European exploration along the Gulf Coast in what is now known as the southern United States. During this period, chiefdoms were established by mound building. In the heart of the Mobile River Delta lies the Bottle Creek site, still visible only by boat to this day. Bottle Creek was the center of the Pensacola Chiefdom, a political and religious center for the tribes in this area. The Pensacola Chiefdom is a bit of a misnomer. What we know today as the Mobile-Tensaw Delta was the epicenter of this culture, not our sister city of Pensacola to the east. Nevertheless, eighteen mounds, some as high as eighty-one feet, dotted the area. Bottle Creek was home to over two thousand people, making it one of the largest communities during this time.

Dr. Greg Waselkov, former director of the University of South Alabama Center for Archaeological Studies, believes the eighty-one-foot structure took about one hundred years to build in stages using woven baskets of clay and clam shells. Since 1991, the Alabama Museum of Natural History has conducted excavations at the Bottle Creek site. Excavations have found at the top of these mounds evidence of large amounts of meat, vegetables and shellfish. The chiefdom leaders and ruling class would have occupied the tallest mounds. They had finer cuts of meat, ample amounts of corn and larger shellfish than the lower class below. Cultivation of the three sisters—maize, beans and squash—dominated the diet of that time. White-tailed deer, black bear and buffalo were hunted. Deer and animal skins clothed and sheltered them in the wintertime. Primarily the women worked the fields. Women also did a majority of the planting, harvesting and cooking while men hunted and gathered.

Their food supply had improved, and the population increased; this allowed more people to hone their pottery skills and not be hunters and gathers full time. Pots, tools and ceremonial objects are still admired today by discoverers. Pottery found on the site show us the many cooking jars, plates and bowls used at mealtime.

The location of Bottle Creek enabled them to harvest from local freshwater creeks, brackish waters of what is now Mobile Bay and the salt water from the Gulf of Mexico, where they brought back shellfish from the coast. The Indigenous people of this area didn't know at the time they were living in the second-largest river delta system on the continent, but evidence at one site along the Mobile River, the skeleton of an adult male from this period, has shown that these people were well fed, strong and healthy. Research shows that 80 percent of their diet came from the local waters. Nets were cast to bring in fish like bass and croaker. Traps were set for catfish and gar. Spears were used for flounder and mullet. Shrimp were harvested using nets woven from fibers of Spanish moss and palmetto fronds. Women and children contributed by scooping clams, oysters and mussels into hand-woven baskets. Turtle, duck, opossum and squirrel were also a part of a consistent diet. Canebrakes along the shore of the Mobile River provided materials for their houses, baskets and fishhooks. Palmetto branches were used as to create sheltering roofs. Walls were made of wooden tree posts.

The people of this time relied solely on their crops for survival. Regular flooding along the Mobile River in the spring months ensured a soft, fertile ground to cultivate beans, squash and especially corn. Corn was the main component of their diets. The Indians ate corn raw, boiled or roasted over a flame on a pile of wooden sticks. They ground the corn into meal for flour and grits. Corn provided a foundation for beer and whiskey. Dried corn was stored in elevated cribs to last throughout the winter. Corn lasted through the winter and was vital to their survival. Corn might have been the single most important thing that ensured their survival, but not far behind were oysters.

The natives solely relied on a diet of corn and oysters. Evidence of their reliance on oysters can still be found today at Dauphin Island, Alabama. Dauphin Island is a small island located thirty-five miles south of Mobile. Shell Mound Park is located on the northern stretch of the island and is its highest point. Recent archaeological explorations have uncovered the mounds are made solely of oyster shells and fish bones from discarded meals. Some twenty feet high, the mounds are also believed to have helped keep the Natives high above sea level and protect them against enemy attack.

Oysters are not only important to our diet as Mobilians but also equally vital to our ecosystem. All of our native reefs in Mobile Bay are gone. Due to an unrestricted harvest, we completely ate almost all of the oysters out of Mobile Bay. In 1888, the first year of record, 120 million pounds of oysters were harvested. New technology at the time allowed workers to use dredges to drag the floor of Mobile Bay and reach oysters that tongs could not. Oysters were supplied in ample amounts during this time, but the bounty came at a significant cost. Mobile Bay would see a decline of 98 percent a century later. Ben Raines, formerly of AL.com, estimates that nearly 1.8 billion oysters have been removed from Mobile Bay over the last century. The unrestricted harvest ended in 2011. Now reefs are only open for harvest when the reef is healthy enough to supply that harvest. Wintzell's Oyster House uses a program through the Alabama Coastal Foundation that recycles the 182,000 pounds of oysters consumed each year inside the restaurant. Oyster shells are picked up each week, then sit outside in the sun for six months for Mother Nature to remove any remaining residue from the shell before being returned back to the Alabama waters.

A visit to Mobile is not complete without a visit to the oyster bar stools of Wintzell's Oyster House, housed inside the oldest wood frame commercial building in the Lower Dauphin Street Historic District, dating back to 1892. Wintzell's became a popular destination for tourists with the six thousand quotes and hand-painted signs on the wall. Oliver Wintzell could spot a

FOUNDATIONS OF FLAVOR

Hand-painted signs with the humor of J. Oliver Wintzell adorn the walls at Wintzell's Oyster House. *Library of Congress.*

tourist every time. While most Mobilians would come in and eat two or three dozen oysters in a sitting, an out-of-towner would "usually only settle for a dozen," according to Wintzell.

Today, hungry patrons enjoy a lot more than just raw oysters on the menu. The Wintzell family gumbo has been annually named the best in town by *Mobile Bay* magazine, the Nappie Awards presented by *Lagnaippe* and the Taste of Mobile. Wintzell's gumbo does not contain okra like most do. Instead, Wintzell's gumbo is made with sassafras leaves ground to become filé, which gives the gumbo a unique, delicious flavor. Fresh Gulf seafood like red snapper, flounder and shrimp, along with po-boys, fried dill pickles and an oyster sampler, fill the menu. The oyster sampler is an alternative to raw oysters. The sampler includes many different flavored oysters like the Oysters Monterrey with bacon, cheddar cheese and a jalapeño or the Oyster Rockefeller with spinach and mozzarella cheese.

Wintzell's Dauphin Street location summons a lot of nostalgic memories from many Mobilians. The location has also seen its fair share of celebrities and notable guests. Willard Scott named Wintzell's "The Best Oysters and Crabs" in his *All-American Cookbook*. In 2007, chef and creator of the show *Bizarre Foods* Andrew Zimmern made a stop by Wintzell's on a Gulf Coast episode that featured the fried dill pickles as a bizarre delicacy. Wintzell's was even selected by former president George W. Bush and former first lady Laura Bush to cater a meal on Air Force One.

Going back many decades, J. Oliver Wintzell has offered an oyster eating contest for eager patrons. To attempt the record, anyone can show up and, in one hour, eat more than the current record holder while sitting at the Wintzell's oyster bar. The winner is awarded a $25 check (inflation not considered) and their name added to the wall of champions. In 2010, the Wintzell's oyster eating record was broken by Ken Orndoff of Hoover, Alabama. Ken visited Mobile often on work trips, and he would take his clients to Wintzell's for lunch. One day, he saw the oyster eating contest record sign and decided that he could break the record of 403. On September 11, 2010, Ken sat down at the famous oyster bar and began his quest. He consumed 421 raw oysters in just thirty-four minutes. His name is forever etched on the walls of Wintzell's Oyster House along with his $25 check and picture on the front page of the next day's *Mobile Press Register*.

Each year, the annual Distinguished Young Women contest is held in Mobile. A young lady from each state is selected to participate to compete for scholarships and college tuition. While the contest is centered on the young women and their interview skills, fitness, talent and other forms of self-expression, all of that is placed aside for five minutes each year as the Distinguished Young Women have an oyster eating contest at Wintzell's Oyster House on their agenda. The reactions from some are shock and disgust at their first oyster, but others take the challenge head-on, such as Jimmienell Morgan, who was Miss New Mexico in 2013. She set the record by consuming eighty raw oysters.

That famous oyster bar, which saw its first oyster shucked in the middle of the Great Depression by Oliver Wintzell, now holds the name of the most famous man to ever shuck oysters behind that bar. His name is Willie Brown, an icon behind the oyster bar for over forty-seven years at Wintzell's Oyster House and hired by Mr. Wintzell himself. Willie's shucking craft over the decades was unmatched, and a countless number of Mobilians had their first bivalve from his hands. Brown worked there until his death in

At Wintzell's Oyster House, an oyster eating contest is open for any to attempt. Ken Orndoff holds the record for 421 oysters eaten in one hour. *Author's collection, 2019.*

2017, when Wintzell's appropriately named the oyster bar Willie's Oyster Bar. A visit to Willie's Oyster Bar includes a large portrait of Willie Brown shucking oysters in that very location. There is also a shadowbox of memorabilia like his name tag, apron and oyster shucking knife from his days shucking oysters behind the bar. At his funeral, Mobile mayor Sandy Stimpson wrote about Brown, "If Mobile is an oyster, Willie was our pearl."

Behind the oyster bar, you'll find the first sign hung by Mr. Wintzell: "A man can sometimes get a pearl out of an oyster, but it takes a pretty girl to get a diamond out of an old crab." J. Oliver Wintzell found that people in Mobile love to eat oysters in good times and bad. People have been living here for thousands of years and enjoying the oysters of this area, long before Mr. Wintzell began serving them and long before the French arrived to settle the city of Mobile. We will be eating oysters in Mobile for as long as our waters will produce them. The versatile oyster, much like the city itself, has played a vital role in shaping Mobile's identity and sense of place.

2
INKING THE PAST

THE FOUNDING OF MOBILE AND SQUID INK

"We put real food in our food" has been a motto of Chef Pete Blohme's restaurants in the Mobile area since he opened his first restaurant, Panini Pete's, located in Fairhope, Alabama, in 2006. At Squid Ink Eclectic Eats and Drinks, Pete's gastropub at historic 102 Dauphin Street, they put real history in their food too.

Menu items at Squid Ink represent the six flags that have flown over Mobile throughout its history. French, British, Spanish, American, State of Alabama and Confederate flags have all flown over Mobile since its beginning in 1702. At Squid Ink, you'll find nods to these periods of history on the menu all in one setting. Paella fritters represent Mobile's Spanish history spanning from 1780 to 1812, fish and chips represent the British period of Mobile from 1760 to 1780, the "Damn the Torpedoes" cocktail is a nod to Mobile's Confederate period of 1861 to 1864 and the Cadillac Burger represents the French period of colonial Mobile from 1702 to 1760.

In search of El Dorado and the Seven Cities of Gold, the Spanish began settling along the Gulf of Mexico: La Florida in 1513, Havana, Cuba in 1515, Veracruz in 1519 and soon Mobile Bay. Álvarez de Pineda is believed to be the first European to chart the waters of the Mobile River and Mobile Bay. The next 175 years would see Spanish explorers come and go along the waters of Mobile. The Bottle Creek chiefdom came to an end during this time. Descendants of the Pensacola Chiefdom still lived along the banks of the thirty-one-mile-long river. These descendants were known as the Mabilla tribe of Indians. The Mabilians, derived from the Choctaw word *moeli*, meaning "to paddle," were a tribe of approximately three hundred when the French arrived in 1699. First landing on modern-day Dauphin Island, the French arrived at a small quiet island with piles of dead bodies, bones and various utensils staring back at them. The explorers were certain that savages were responsible for the deaths, so they dubbed it Massacre Island.

The leaders of the French explorers were two brothers, Pierre LeMoyne Sieur D'Iberville and Jean-Baptiste LeMoyne Sieur de Bienville. D'Iberville and Bienville were commissioned by King Louis XIV of France to explore the northern Gulf Coast and build a series of forts and settlements along the Gulf Coast and Mississippi River, thus known as Louisiana. The French desired a trade route from Canada to the Gulf of Mexico. D'Iberville was the leader of the group. He was a military and war hero in New France throughout the seventeenth century, now tasked with building a fort at the mouth of the Mississippi River so that only France would control the commerce from the river. The group traveled the shores of the northern Gulf for years searching for a permanent settlement. Finally, in 1702, a permanent settlement was established twenty-seven miles north of where the Mobile River dumps into Mobile Bay. A small wooden fort was built with four ramparts to protect the new town, Fort Louisiane de la Mobile. D'Iberville left the colony in 1702 and never returned. He contracted an illness and in 1706 died of yellow fever in Havana, Cuba, where he still lies at the Church of San Cristobal. Bienville, then twenty-three years old, became governor of the colony.

Once the French began to settle, the Mabila tribe saw an opportunity to grow their tribe by using the French to defend them in war against the hostile Alabamian tribe. They also saw trade with the French as vital to their growth. The French, in turn, also saw a great benefit from befriending the Mabilas. Deerskins and fur were in high demand back in Europe. At the time, Europeans prized deerskins for making gloves, hats, saddles and book covers. Deerskins were also used to make clothing. Pants of the eighteenth century made from deerskins were equivalent to a modern-day pair of Levi's. The French also traded pipes for tobacco and firearms in exchange for necessities like deer meat and woven baskets.

Many men in the colony were young and reckless. They saw the frontier along the Gulf Coast as an opportunity to express and pursue an adventurous lifestyle. They learned from the Mabilas how to hunt and fish. They learned what vegetables grew well and they learned about corn. Oysters were a

A view from the bluff at the Old Mobile site overlooking the Mobile River. *Author's collection, 2016.*

primary source of their diet. They harvested oysters from the Mobile River and Mobile Bay. A few shops lined the sandy and muddy roads of the town along with, of course, taverns, where the first Mardi Gras celebration occurred there in 1703. The scent in the air of the early town was a mixture of human and animal waste, wood smoke, pine tar and rotting fish. The colony was stagnant in more ways than the smell. Economically, Bienville feared an insurrection between the men, and trade voyages bringing supplies from France were slow and undependable due to delays in supply ships. Bienville saw a need to grow the colony with women. In 1704, Bienville wrote to King Louis XIV, "If you want to make something of this country, it is absolutely necessary to send this year some families and a few girls… who will be married off shortly after arrival." King Louis granted Bienville his wish. Twenty-three young French girls were selected to travel to the New World. Most of the girls were teenagers who came from convents and orphanages around France. They were promised a utopian new world with a chance to be courted by the French Canadian men.

In 1704, the girls arrived aboard the *Le Pelican*, thus forever making them known as the Pelican Girls. Some of them carried a casquette with their belongings, marking them the Cassette or Casket Girls. These casquettes carried the girls' only belongings. One other thing some of them were unknowingly carrying was disease. The girls contracted yellow fever during a stop in Cuba, which spread throughout the colony, killing dozens upon their arrival. The girls must have been disappointed to find the paradise they were promised in France was not a land of milk and honey when they arrived. Instead, they had been brought to a new world of backwoods, disease and hardship. Despite these circumstances, the girls did marry the men and begin to grow the colony. However, the men were more interested in being a *coureur de bois*, or "runner of the woods." They traded with the Natives in exchange for fur and animal skins. To make matters worse, most of the men were more interested in the young Native women than the Pelican Girls.

By 1706, the women had been reduced to a diet of corn and acorns and finally had enough. They rebelled against Bienville and the men over the deplorable living conditions in Mobile. Many of the women demanded a return to France. Ultimately, their grievances were appeased but not without angering Bienville and the leaders. It's possible the Petticoat Insurrection of 1706 was technically the very first women's rights movement in North America.

One notable man in the colony of Mobile at 27 Mile Bluff was a colonist named François Lemesle. Not much is documented of Lemesle's time in Mobile except that he was a baker. Flour was a staple in Europe but had to be imported to Mobile during those days. Most breads at the time were made from corn or wheat. The French got creative and ground the corn into flour, which became a source of bread for the colony. In 1722, Lemesle moved to the new city of New Orleans—also founded by

Historical markers at 27 Mile Bluff, Mobile's original site, commemorate the city's bicentennial in 1902 and tercentennial in 2002. *Author's collection, 2016.*

Bienville and the French—located less than 150 miles to the west. There in New Orleans, François Lemesle founded the Bellegarde Bakery in the French Quarter, at the corner of St. Ann and Chartres Streets. It was the first bakery in a town that is now known throughout the world for its use of bread in po-boys, beignets, muffulettas and king cakes. The original Bellegarde Bakery lasted only a few years, but the contributions to that city's food scene are esteemed. It is also correct to assume that during his time in Mobile baking bread, Lemesle entertained, if not executed, the idea of the first oyster loaf, seafood po-boy or cake in North America before spreading those ideas to the Crescent City, where the dishes would later become iconic in American food culture.

Bienville had built an impeccable relationship with the Natives in the area. His knowledge of the woods, wilderness and waters was unmatched. Meanwhile, in France, the French were engaged in the War of Spanish Succession, further delaying men, material and resources the colony needed to survive. Bienville helped the colony survive the lean first decade of Mobile's eighteenth-century history, but his time as governor would soon come to an end. In 1712, Antoine de la Mothe Cadillac was appointed governor of Louisiana. Cadillac was an expert fur trader and became a prominent figure when he proposed the colonization of Detroit, which would serve the French militarily, economically and culturally. His name would become more prominent in 1902 when a luxury car company was named after him.

Cadillac and Bienville were consistently at odds during their time in Mobile. First, they disagreed over the fact that Bienville was replaced as governor, and Bienville was even more upset that Cadillac showed little to no regard for the Natives—relationships that Bienville had worked hard to secure. Cadillac was dismissive of the four hundred or so people living in Mobile during his time, even referring to them as "not worth a straw." He found the colony lacking in natural resources. The sandy soil had produced only a handful of fruit trees in Mobile, which led to most of the agriculture being delegated to Dauphin Island and areas south of Mobile, all while commerce was at a standstill. "They know nothing of cultivated silk, tobacco, or indigo, but only corn and vegetables," complained Cadillac. Although he was not a religious man and, in fact, was hostile toward the local Jesuits and their missionaries, Cadillac ordered the closing of all taverns due to excessive drinking. One missionary described him as "a man without faith, without religion, without honor and without conscience." Additionally, he ordered the men to stop wearing swords and refused to smoke a peace pipe with the Natives.

Cadillac's days as governor came to an end in 1717, but not without controversy. Cadillac was accused by the French government of personally profiting from Louisiana. He left Mobile in 1717 for France and never returned. He was subsequently thrown in the Bastille prison for making false accusations against the French government and its colonies. Bienville assumed the role of interim governor and went on to found New Orleans in 1718. This, after founding Biloxi and a fort that would later become Natchez.

The stark contrast of legacies between Bienville and Cadillac is evident today. Bienville's name was honored by Mobilians as the namesake of the city's first park and town square, Bienville Square. Antoine de la Mothe Cadillac has been mostly forgotten through the annals of Mobile history; a small plaque on Conti Street that tells of his nearby home that once stood is all that remains—that is, until Squid Ink opened its doors. Upon entering the hip, eclectic doors of Squid Ink, the first thing you'll notice is the wall of an assortment of decades-old Cadillac rims and hubcaps and a small plaque in the center. The signature burger is the Cadillac Burger, French inspired with Brie cheese and bacon shallot jam, and the bar offers a Pink Cadillac cocktail.

Antoine de la Mothe
CADILLAC
Soldier of Fortune
Lover of Good Food & Drink
Founder of Detroit, Name sake of
The Cadillac Automobile
Lived very near here acting as
The Royal Gov. Of French Louisiana
In the early 1700's when Mobile was
The Capital of French Louisiana

The building at 102 Dauphin Street has been many different restaurants through the decades. It was originally an oyster bar back in the 1880s. The Palace Café operated here in the 1930s and was the city's first air-conditioned restaurant. Squid Ink opened in 2019 as a gastropub, an eclectic restaurant serving a collection of some of the best burgers in Mobile, along with sandwiches and unique dishes like Spanish S.O.S (Squid on a Shingle), fried deviled eggs or the Tuna Poke Boa and a drink menu that rivals any bar in town. Chef Pete Blohme is our celebrity chef in Mobile; we know him as Panini Pete.

The Cadillac Wall at Squid Ink is a nod to former French governor of Louisiana, Antoine de la Mothe Cadillac who lived in Mobile from 1713 to 1717. *Author's collection, 2021.*

Pete Blohme was born in Chicago but raised in Fort Lauderdale, Florida. At the age of fourteen, young Peter began working in restaurants like Pizza Hut, steakhouses and other popular eateries along the waterfront in Fort Lauderdale. He fell in love with the restaurant industry and decided to take his talents north to the Culinary Institute of America in Hyde Park, New York, where he graduated. He professional career began with stints at hotels, cruise ships and the University of Alabama, where he was executive chef for Aramark.

In 2006, he opened his first restaurant, Panini Pete's, in Fairhope, Alabama. In the French Quarter of Fairhope, Pete opened a scratch kitchen serving sandwiches, paninis and burgers. Everything was made in-house, from the mozzarella to the dressing, fresh-cut fries and even the bread. However, his most popular item on the menu are the beignets. What distinguishes the beignets at Panini Pete's from other places along the Gulf Coast we shall not name is a simple lemon. Pete started making beignets when he realized no one else in Fairhope's French Quarter was making anything similar; it was only fitting that beignets be served in the

Right: Chef Panini Pete greeting a Taste of Fairhope tour group at the landmark Panini Pete's in Fairhope, Alabama. *Nicky Mendenhall, 2021.*

Opposite: A lemon complements the irresistible beignets from Panini Pete's and Squid Ink, served fresh and ready to delight. *Nicky Mendenhall, 2021.*

French Quarter. He tweaked the recipe using a wet dough until he came up with the perfect beignet. These are fluffy, soft and airy. Pete gave away those beignets in the early days to get the support of merchants in the popular shopping district of downtown Fairhope. Six months into serving the beignets, he saw a server cutting lemons for tea and immediately remembered a favorite recipe from childhood. His mother made German pancakes for him as a treat when he was well behaved. Pete says he rarely had them because he almost never behaved. His mother served this rare treat with powdered sugar and lemon squeezed on top. Perfection! Squeezing the lemon on your beignets is a signature of eating beignets along Mobile Bay.

The producers of the now hit show from the Food Network *Diners, Drive Ins and Dives* contacted Panini Pete early in the show's history. Though he originally thought it was a prank, the crews showed up to film and the show aired, which gave Pete national exposure but most importantly a friendship with host Guy Fieri. That friendship completely changed the trajectory of Pete's restaurant business. Guy proclaimed his house roasted turkey sandwich as the "State Bird of Flavortown"—Flavortown has turned into a world of its own from Guy's success on the Food Network. It is a world that is home to the best dishes, iconic food and unforgettable eateries. That endorsement has sent Food Network fans from all over the world to Fairhope, Alabama, to experience Panini Pete's. It was also Guy's idea to create a network of celebrity chefs to travel across the world feeding American troops on submarines and aircraft carriers. They put on cooking classes and have live concerts for the troops serving abroad. Panini Pete was a founding member of that group, called the Messlords.

Pete later expanded Panini Pete's to a second location in downtown Mobile, where he would soon occupy the building at 102 Dauphin Street. The successful eatery was a hit with the lunch crowd downtown. Despite the success, Pete decided to transition Panini Pete's in Mobile to Squid Ink Eclectic Eats and Drinks in 2019. Squid Ink is a nod, not only to the ingredient, which appears in many dishes and cocktails on the menu, but also to tattoo culture, which Pete is a fan of. During the transition, the historic building got a fresh update, but Pete also included nods to the former restaurants located in that building: Panini Pete's, Little Kitchen, Tanner's Kwik Lunch, Clifton's and the Palace Sandwich Shop. Murals with quotes from famous Mobilians like Jimmy Buffett, Hank Aaron and Satchel Paige also adorn the walls. The menu also transitioned to an eclectic array of dishes to accommodate a growing scene of young people who frequent the Lower Dauphin Street Historic District in the evenings looking for a great meal in a fun environment. You'll even find sushi and poke bowls and Chicken Bahn Mi Bao.

When Pete is not on the Food Network competing on shows like *Guy's Grocery Games* or cooking Paella Fritters served at Squid Ink—also featured on *Diners, Drive-Ins and Dives*—you can find him working in one of his many restaurants in the Mobile area. Squid Ink holds a soft spot for Panini Pete because of his love for history that has infused the menu. The food and drink are so good at Squid Ink, even the grumpy Cadillac himself might finally find pleasure in this town that he so despised.

3

STIRRING THE POT OF HISTORY

THE ROYAL SCAM'S GUMBO AND COLONIAL MOBILE

Sooner or later all Southerners come home, not to die, but to eat gumbo.
—*Eugene Walter*

From the earliest days of Mobile as a struggling outpost, its residents have made the most of the region's abundant natural resources and forged a unique cuisine that reflects their resilience and creativity. Mobile was a struggling outpost colony at the beginning of 1711. Flooding had occurred at the 27 Mile Bluff, Old Mobile site, causing much disease and hardship in the colony. The French government was inept and near bankrupt. Jean Baptiste LeMoyne D'Bienville began looking for new locations to move the town. He settled on a large bluff on the western shore of the Mobile River, near where its mouth empties into Mobile Bay. This location was strategic, being situated at the mouth of one of the largest river systems in North America. Work soon began to grow the town, build a new fort and lay out the grid for the city's streets. Many of these streets are still in use today and occupy today's central business and entertainment district of downtown Mobile: Royal Street, St. Francis Street and Dauphin Street, to name a few.

The first fort built on the modern-day location of Mobile was a second iteration of the original Fort Louis. The French originally used cedar to build the fort and soon found that wood structures don't last long in one of the rainiest cities on this continent. In 1720, Fort Conde de la Mobile was constructed of locally made bricks and earthen walls. The fort was a four-pointed star design with bastions that measured over three hundred feet.

The only remains of Colonial Mobile are found in these ruins along Church Street in Mobile. *Author's collection, 2021.*

Cannons were used to protect the brick structure. A moat surrounded the walls for further protection, and a passage on the east end led a few hundred feet to the Mobile River. Inside the fort, barracks held over two hundred men, a magazine for gunpowder and artillery, a kitchen, a dining room and three wells.

Just outside the north wall of where the fort once stood now stands a small restaurant along Royal Street called The Royal Scam. Owned and operated by David Rasp since 2006, The Royal Scam is one of Mobile's most popular eateries. The restaurant is a play on words from its location along Alabama's oldest street, Royal Street, and the popular Steely Dan song and album from the 1970s, *The Royal Scam*. The Royal Scam serves some of the best-tasting entrees in Mobile, with certified Angus steaks, pork chops and chicken; this restaurant is anything but what its name suggests, a scam. Also found on the menu is arguably Mobile's best seafood gumbo. (No argument from this author but maybe to some.) A trip to Mobile without a cup of seafood gumbo would be like going to Philadelphia and not having a Philly cheesesteak or a visit to New Orleans without a beignet. The Royal Scam does it as well as anybody in Mobile.

No dish encapsulates Mobile's history like seafood gumbo. It's a melting pot of a dish that represents a melding of different cultures. Gumbo is derived from the African word for okra, making it the primary ingredient for any cup of gumbo. This dish, also known as kombo in the native Choctaw language, reflects the word for sassafras trees. Many of these trees still grow wild along the Mobile River today. The first bowl of gumbo was likely served in Mobile on dishware from Mexico or China with okra acquired from the West Indies, seafood from the Mobile River, peppers from the Caribbean, filé from the Natives and a roux from a mixture of fat, flour and oil browned over an open flame. While okra is a primary ingredient for gumbo, fresh seafood is just as important. This includes shrimp, crab, fish, oysters or any shellfish that is readily available fresh.

Oysters continue to be vital to the diets of Mobile's first residents, much like they were before the Europeans arrived. Oysters were also vital to Mobilians as an architectural tool. The first roads in Mobile were all paved using oyster shells. Oyster shells were burned to extract lime, then mixed with sand and water; more broken shells were added and mixed to create a form of concrete called tabby. Foundations of the first buildings were made of tabby. A lot of the early buildings were plastered from oyster shells to help fortify homes from the muggy Gulf Coast climate. Most of the first homes were wood frame houses with double pitched roofs that sat above the ground on blocks.

Most residents had a small garden and poultry to consume. The conditions were never pleasant. A constant scent of human and animal waste along with rotting fish and woodsmoke permeated the city. The physical conditions were stagnant along with the economic conditions of Mobile throughout the

French period. Wars in Europe and continued delays in shipping supplies from Europe continued to hamper growth in the colony.

In 1763, the Treaty of Paris was signed, effectively ending the French and Indian War. The treaty placed Mobile into British hands, and it became a part of British West Florida, which spanned from the Apalachicola River to the east where it joined British East Florida to the Mississippi River and Baton Rouge to the west. British West Florida went no farther south than Lake Pontchartrain, which excluded New Orleans from being a part of the British colony. Some residents of Mobile moved to French-controlled New Orleans at this time so as not to be a part of the "fourteenth colony" of British West Florida and subjects of King George III, but a majority of them did stay.

Conditions in Mobile did improve some during British reign. First, the British renamed Fort Conde to Fort Charlotte, in honor of the queen of England. The population was around 350 at the time. The town consisted of around one dozen businesses, livestock roaming through the muddy streets and wooden homes that could be considered nothing more than huts. The warm, tropical climate continually made it difficult for residents to sustain wooden homes that were susceptible to the heavy rains and occasional hurricanes along the Gulf Coast. Upon his arrival to Mobile in 1764, British general Robert Farmer described its appearance as "a little hamlet formed of Negro Huts, rather than a well populated town in Canada." Despite the underwhelming attitude from Farmer, Mobile was British West Florida's largest town and its central location. Along with Pensacola, the two towns served as the prized possessions of British West Florida. Food was scarce in Mobile but even more so in Pensacola, where the sandy soil prevented the locals there from growing abundant gardens. For the first decade of British reign, troops in Pensacola were supplied food and vegetables from Mobile.

Largely untouched from any sort of military conflict throughout the Revolutionary War period, Mobile and British West Florida frequently dealt with the threat of invasion by American troops and the Spanish. The British left the Gulf Coast vulnerable to attack while war was waging in the thirteen original colonies. The Americans sought to add Florida and the Mississippi River to the colonies while the Spanish wanted to reaffirm their dominance along the Gulf Coast. In addition to controlling New Orleans, much like it had in the sixteenth and seventeenth centuries, Spain sought full control of the Gulf at one point with cities like Vera Cruz, Havana and the entire coast from modern-day Florida to Texas. While American takeover was nothing more than rumor, the Spanish were successful in a military takeover

Mobile's evolution through the centuries, from eighteenth-century Fort Conde to the twenty-first-century RSA Tower, masterfully captured in one frame. *Author's collection, 2020.*

of Mobile. In 1780, General Bernardo de Galvez overwhelmed the small number of British troops at Fort Charlotte over four to one, led at the time by interim governor, Elias Durnford. The walls were eventually breached by Spanish gunfire but not before a strange exchange of gifts between Galvez and Durnford. Durnford sent Galvez a number of chickens, bread, bottles of wine and a lamb. In return, Galvez gifted Durnford with his own bottle of wine, oranges, tea biscuits, corn cakes and Cuban cigars. Despite the kind exchange between the two, Galvez pressured Durnford for two weeks until the white flag was raised over Fort Charlotte. Soon after, the Spanish raised their flag and renamed the fort Fuerta Carlota. The Spanish now controlled Louisiana and Mobile with their sights set on Pensacola to claim dominance on the Gulf Coast.

The colonial period of Mobile was a continuous struggle economically. Primarily, Mobilians were farmers. Corn was the main food source for many in the area. They also planted vegetables like asparagus, cucumbers, tomatoes, beans, peans, carrots, onions, cabbage, turnips and pumpkins in local gardens. Fruits like watermelon, peaches and oranges grew in abundance. Wild berries, muscadine grapes and strawberries were gathered. Hunting wild game such as deer and turkey was common. Those who had

The Royal Scam presents a delectable bowl of its signature seafood gumbo. *Author's collection, 2021.*

access fished in the nearby streams. Meals consisted of stews from vegetables and seafood like gumbo. Seafood gumbos in Mobile have evolved from makeshift meals to fine delicacies in the centuries since.

Rasp opened the doors at 72 South Royal Street primarily to accommodate the large number of guests who stayed in hotels along Royal Street like the historic Battle House Hotel, which has been open on Royal Street since the 1850s. A century later, the hotel now known as the Renaissance Riverview Plaza Hotel is directly across the street from The Royal Scam. In the late 2000s, a Hampton Inn opened in the same block as the restaurant at Royal and Conti. These travelers soon find out what the locals already know, and that's the treasure of a restaurant that The Royal Scam is.

Although the acclaimed seafood gumbo often takes the spotlight on the menu, loyal patrons highly recommend other appetizers such as the tuna tartare—ahi tuna marinated in a soy sesame blend, garnished with cucumber, onion, tomato, a crispy wonton, and wasabi crème fraîche. Also, the delectable Gulf crab cakes drizzled with a sriracha-lemon aioli and the Hanoi shrimp, a Vietnamese-inspired dish served with green rice and a soy garlic chili sauce, are not to be missed.

Gumbos like the ones served at The Royal Scam are an authentic old Mobile dining experience. Even the atmosphere inside is an old Mobile experience with exposed brick on the walls, and for outdoor dining, it is one of the most charming courtyards in Mobile. If a restaurant existed in Mobile during its colonial period, the menu would have looked much like the one from The Royal Scam three centuries later: fresh fish, beef, asparagus, potatoes, duck, pork, shrimp and cabbage for salads and, of course, gumbo. Steely Dan sang these words thirty years before the doors opened at 72 North Royal Street, but the words still ring true nonetheless, "See the glory of The Royal Scam."

PART II
HARVEST AND HARDSHIP

THE INTERSECTION OF HISTORY AND FOOD IN MOBILE'S NINETEENTH CENTURY

4

FROM OYSTER SALOONS TO OAKLEIGH

CALLAGHAN'S IRISH SOCIAL CLUB AND THE CULINARY LANDSCAPE OF MOBILE IN THE 1800s

*F*ollowing the Creek War and the War of 1812, twenty-three million acres of land was ceded by the Native Americans. Major General Andrew Jackson demanded the Creeks give up their land based on the fact that they incited the war to begin with. The Creek chiefs agreed, and on signing the terms, an outpouring of people arrived to this new American land. People from South Carolina, Tennessee and states throughout the Southeast came to this new frontier of land once called the Mississippi Territory. The Mississippi Territory encompassed modern-day Mississippi and Alabama. The large land mass was split in 1817 when Mississippi became a state. In 1819, the eastern portion of that land mass became a state, Alabama.

At this time, Mobile was a sleepy and struggling outpost of around 1,000 people. Fort Conde was nearly desolate. A yellow fever epidemic had decimated almost half of the town's population. Mostly French, Spanish and Creole inhabitants occupied the area. That soon was about to change. Settlers in Alabama began to grow cotton on this new frontier of land. Once the cotton was picked, cotton was floated downriver via the Tombigbee, Alabama and Mobile Rivers, eventually ending up in Mobile. By 1820, Fort Conde had been demolished, its ruins used to fill land between Royal Street and the Mobile River. Eventually, a new road was made—Water Street. Improvements began on Mobile's waterfront, and by 1822, six wharves had been built with more under construction. Warehouses soon lined the waterfront along with stores, office buildings, coffee saloons, oyster houses, bakeries, a fish market and hardware stores. Within a decade, trade with Havana, Cuba, flourished after U.S. investors began to purchase Cuban plantations. Ships brought sugar, coffee, pineapples, molasses and rum from

Cuba to Mobile. Ship traffic had steadily increased and so did the amount of cotton coming through the town. More settlers were farming the land dozens to hundreds of miles north of Mobile using chattel slavery, and bales of cotton, thousands of pounds—eventually millions of pounds—of cotton were coming down the Mobile River to the Port City. Mobile became the third-busiest port in the United States by 1860, trailing behind New Orleans and New York City. Cotton in Mobile was sent across the Atlantic to Europe or up the Eastern Seaboard to New York City—the ships never came back to Mobile empty. The first coffee in the state of Alabama came from the port during this time along with fine china, silverware and other household luxuries. The Mobile economy thrived. Many of our finest buildings standing today were built in antebellum Mobile—Barton Academy, the Cathedral Basilica of the Immaculate Conception, Government Street Presbyterian Church and the Oakleigh Mansion, just to name a few.

The first restaurants in Mobile appeared in the 1830s. The South Coffee House "Restaurat" was located on the busy waterfront along Water Street between Conti and Government. Edmund Pouchet and Company advertised a French-style restaurant serving breakfasts, dinners and suppers at all hours. It would even fill orders for soirees and balls as well as serving pastries and confections. Pouchet also had another establishment at 62 Commerce Street between Conti and Dauphin Streets. The Commerce Street Exchange, "where will be served up all choice sorts of Eatables, and Nick-Nacks the market affords. The Bar is supplied with the best of Wines, and all other kinds of Liquors and Cordials, attended by capable and active men. Oysters, Relishes, and Snacks, &c, served up at all hours at short notice." In 1839, Polly Collins, a free woman of color, operated out of her home at 39 Church Street offering coffee and chocolate "at all reasonable hours, day or night, in first rate style." Polly Collins also kept a full supply of fruits, cakes, cigars, tobacco and even ice cream in the summer for her guests. At 219 Dauphin Street, William Hutchinson opened an oyster house where fresh oysters were always kept day and night to serve customers. The Union House and Dining Saloon at 12 Front Street served Mobilians raw oysters, broiled oysters, fried oysters, stewed oysters, roasted oysters, and pickled oysters. According to advertisements in the *Mobile Press*, you could purchase oysters by the barrel or "put up fresh for spiced in cans of order." Oysters of every variety, like those one could find at the Union House and Dining Saloon, along with oyster soups and oyster stews dominated the menus of Mobile's first restaurants.

Luxurious hotels such as the Waverly, Mansion House or Battle House offered a fine array of meals for their guests. At the Battle House Hotel,

Oyster houses and oyster saloons proudly advertise fresh oysters from Mobile Bay to hungry patrons. *Library of Congress.*

breakfast was served from 7:00 to 10:00 a.m., lunch at 3:00 p.m., tea from 6:30 p.m. to 9:00 p.m. and dinner from 9:00 p.m. to 11:00 p.m. An 1857 menu from the Battle House describes a menu full of boiled meats like redfish, ham, corned beef and cabbage, turkey and corned tongue. Side dishes include boiled hominy, sirloin of beef, curry of beef and calf's head. Roasted meats like beef, chicken, turkey, pork and veal were served with a choice of pudding or pastries like peach pies, huckleberry pies or baked sago pudding. A large assortment of nearly one hundred wines such as Madeira, sherry, Champagne, brandy and sauterne filled the menu.

James Roper was a brick mason, dry-goods merchant and cotton broker who moved to antebellum Mobile from James City, Virginia. Roper operated a brickyard in Mobile where the current RSA Tower stands. In 1833, he began construction on his home on thirty-five acres outside of the city limits of Mobile. James helped design the home while enslaved laborers built it. Oakleigh was completed in 1838. James Roper would not enjoy the fruits of his and the enslaved labor before he was forced to sell the home following the Panic of 1837. Today, the Oakleigh House and Museum wonderfully interprets antebellum Mobile life and society. Surrounding the historic

Greek Revival Oakleigh mansion now sits a thriving neighborhood of historic homes and ancient live oaks, the Oakleigh Garden District, known to the locals as simply Oakleigh.

Inside the Oakleigh Garden District on the corner of Marine and Charleston Streets sits one of the culinary gems of Mobile, Alabama— Callaghan's Irish Social Club. Since 1946, this neighborhood restaurant and bar has been the landmark of this historic neighborhood, not the home it's named after. Woodrow Callaghan opened his restaurant adjacent to his home. Patrons can still dine inside Woodrow's dining room on the original tables. When guests come to Callaghan's though, it's usually for two things: beer and a burger. Their cheeseburgers are iconic, especially the bacon cheeseburger that is served with delicious applewood smoked bacon. Locals will also convince you to never pass up the L.A. Burger; it stands for "Lower Alabama" but "Lip-smackingly Amazing" could also pass for that abbreviation. The L.A. Burger is an Angus beef patty ground with a south Alabama favorite, Conecuh sausage. If you pass on the burgers, you won't be disappointed. The sandwiches, such as the Rueben or the shrimp po-boy, are great choices. Don't miss the French onion or spinach artichoke dip as well to start your meal. Callaghan's is also one of the best live

The beautiful Oakleigh Mansion sits peacefully among the azalea bushes in the Oakleigh Garden District of Mobile, Alabama. *Library of Congress.*

The delicious bacon cheeseburger from Callaghan's Irish Social Club. *Author's collection, 2020.*

music venues found in Mobile. Following Hurricane Katrina in 2005, Callaghan's was a thriving spot for musicians along the Gulf Coast when New Orleans was still recovering from storm damage, and the trend has continued on long since. Inside Callaghan's you'll find a digital clock counting down the days, hours and minutes until St. Patrick's Day—and for good reason. Callaghan's is the epicenter for St. Patrick's Day celebrations in Mobile. The streets are blocked off to traffic while thousands of people gather for green beer, live music and socializing. The party that you will find outside of Callaghan's on St. Patrick's Day is matched only by Mardi Gras in Mobile, further solidifying the fact that Mobile knows how to have a good time.

Holidays have always been marked by abundant feasting in south Alabama. During the antebellum period, holidays, celebrations and harvest times were significant occasions that were enjoyed by both slaveholders and the enslaved. During these events, the traditional food boundaries between White and Black people became less distinct. Hogs were hunted and roasted, chickens were fried and turkeys were served. Enslaved people were treated with gifts of chickens or biscuits on Sundays or after a wedding or special occasion. The development of southern cuisine owes much to the interaction between enslaved Black laborers and plantation owners. Many of the crops that are now emblematic of southern cooking, such as watermelons, pumpkins, rice, sugarcane, cashews, pears, plums and grapes, were grown on Alabama plantations during the antebellum period. Persimmons were used to make beer, while plums were turned into wine, showcasing the resourcefulness and creativity of those who worked the land.

Visitors to Mobile during the antebellum period often viewed the area as lacking refinement, particularly in comparison to the more cultured North. While traveling by steamboat to Mobile in 1854, Frederick Law Olmsted observed that the cotton planters aboard were generally well-dressed but displayed a rough and coarse demeanor, frequently drinking to the point of intoxication. The enslaved individuals aboard the steamboat were forced to dine separately from White passengers on cotton bales, without proper dining utensils. Olmsted noted that the food provided to them was plentiful and varied, including bean porridge, bacon, corn bread, ship's biscuit, potatoes, duff (pudding) and gravy. However, he also remarked that only one knife was shared among ten enslaved people and they used bone splinters and firewood as makeshift forks. The porridge was passed from person to person and consumed directly from the tub.

Shellfish and oysters in particular continued to be the dominant food group of Mobilians throughout the nineteenth century. Mobile Bay was teeming with oysters, shrimp and crab during this time. During the Civil War, soldiers enjoyed the seafood buffet, which satisfied the otherwise starving men. Oysters were so plentiful that men could scoop their hands across the floor of Mobile Bay and find the bivalves. The advent of railroad travel in the nineteenth century began to connect cities across the country like never before. This advancement in transportation also made an impact on the oyster industry in Mobile. Oysters could be canned, packed with ice and sent by rail to places like Chicago or St. Louis in a couple of days. Fresh oysters from Mobile Bay could now be enjoyed at saloons and bars by people in the Midwest, something that would have been unthinkable decades prior.

Mobile continued to be a melting pot of people in the nineteenth century. Descendants of French, Spanish, British and American settlers lived in the town along with enslaved and free Blacks, Creoles, inhabitants of Europe and natives from the North all together made Mobile one of, if not the most, diverse cities in the United States. As a result, dishes on the tables reflected that diversity.

The first and oldest known recipe for jambalaya is found inside the *Gulf City Cook Book*, which was published by the women of the St. Francis Street Methodist Church in 1878. We find the first mention of the word *jambalaya* in print dating back to 1849. Solon Robinson was a writer and traveled the South during the 1830s and '40s. He submitted his writings to different magazines that would publish his works. In the May 1849 edition of the *American Agriculturalists*, Robinson, writing from Mobile, published three Gulf Coast recipes. "Hopping John (Jambalaya)" was one of the recipes published. It consisted of "taking a dressed chicken or fowl cut into pieces, placed into a pot with a spoonful of butter and a chopped onion." Thirty years later, on page 57 of the *Gulf City Cook Book*, a recipe for "Jam Bolaya" is found using chicken, oysters and tomatoes mixed with rice.

The second-oldest recipe in the United States for jambalaya came from a woman living in San Francisco, California, by the name of Abby Fisher. In 1881, her cookbook *What Mrs. Fisher Knows About Old Southern Cooking* was published. Abby Clifton was born into slavery in South Carolina. Her father was a White farmer born in France, her mother a slave. Abby grew up and later married a man named Alexander Fisher, a minister and native Alabamian. The couple moved to Mobile sometime around 1860. Mrs. Fisher considered herself a "mulatto" born of African and French descent. Abby Fisher, sharing the same descent as Creoles of Mobile, certainly would have fit in socially throughout the 1860s in the Creole culture of the city. This was a time before the laws of Jim Crow and White supremacy dominated the political and social structures of the South. Sometime in the 1870s, the Fisher family moved to San Francisco. While living on the West Coast, Mrs. Fisher was asked by many of her closest friends to share her cooking recipes for a cookbook. Abby Fisher's biggest obstacle in writing her book was that she couldn't read or write. With the help of her friends, 160 recipes were published. One recipe she shared was "Jumberlie—A Creole Dish" using ingredients of chicken, ham and tomatoes. The Californians undoubtedly had a hard time translating the word *jambalaya* from her thick Creole accent. *What Mrs. Fisher Knows About Old Southern Cooking* has gone down in history as one of the most celebrated cookbooks ever written by an African American author.

The oldest mention of the word *jambalaya* and the first two uses of the word in a cookbook both originate from Mobile. While there's no record of when the first jambalaya dish was consumed, Creoles in Mobile were certainly some of the first in America to serve this delicious dish. It would have been unthinkable in nineteenth-century Mobile to not associate the city as a place to find some of the best jambalayas in the United States.

Following the Civil War, the Reconstruction period of Mobile was brutally bleak. Cotton no longer was the cash crop it once was, and the once thriving port was a shell of its former self. The city was facing bankruptcy at one point until federal funds were secured to dig and dredge a ship channel in Mobile Bay that reached all the way to the docks along Mobile. The port was again thriving by the end of the nineteenth century. Banana docks lined the wharves of the Mobile River. Bananas were brought in from Central America from places like Uruguay and Honduras. One unfortunate import during this time was the Brazilian fire ant, which made its way to the United States via Mobile's banana docks. Bananas were seen as a novelty by Americans at the time and certainly to the Mobilians

Men are seen offloading a bounty of bananas from a steamship at Mobile's dedicated banana docks. From here, these tropical fruits journeyed across the Southeast and Midwest via train. *Library of Congress.*

working along the waterfront loading them on to refrigerated boxcars and in warehouses. Bananas were shipped by rail all across the United States from Mobile. The boxcars rarely came back to Mobile empty; grapes, muscadines, watermelons and apples that were somewhat foreign in this climate returned to the city in large numbers, a testament to the way trade and transportation shaped regional foodways in the Mobile area.

By incorporating local flavors and ingredients such as those used on the L.A. Burger and smoked tuna dip, Callaghan's Irish Social Club continues to highlight the regional foodways of Mobile, Alabama. It is no surprise that the restaurant has garnered numerous accolades from esteemed publications, including being named "The South's Best Bar" by *Southern Living*, having the "Best Burger in Alabama" according to *Food + Wine* and being crowned the "South's Favorite Bar" by *Garden & Gun*. These accolades are a testament to the exceptional quality of the food and atmosphere at Callaghan's, which continues to stand out as a truly special destination for locals and visitors alike.

5

FROM CHAINS TO FREEDOM

THE STORY OF KAZOOLA AND
EARLY AFRICAN AMERICAN FOODWAYS

Contributions made by African Americans throughout Mobile's history cannot be understated. African slaves arrived on the shores of the Mobile River shortly after Mobile's founding in 1702. Prior to that, the Native Americans were enslaved to work the fields and construct buildings. The first decade of Mobile's history saw almost 200 slaves. Over 180 of them were Indian men and women and around a dozen Black male and female slaves. The first recorded baptism of the Catholic church in Mobile was a child of color in 1707. Jean Baptiste was a five-year-old slave of African and European descent and is believed to be the godchild of Bienville, Mobile's cofounder. African slavery would soon replace Indian slavery over the next few decades.

Four West African slave ships are documented in the first two decades of Mobile's history. In 1721 alone, three ships arrived in Mobile with slaves from West Africa. The *Africane* carried aboard 240 passengers from Guinea. Only 120 of them survived the voyage. The *Marie* brought 338 from West Africa, and the *Neride* brought 350 from Angola—112 tragically did not survive the voyage. In 1723, the *Expedition* brought 100 Africans from Goree. Despite the rotten conditions, 91 of them miraculously survived. When they arrived, African slaves did the cooking in many wealthy European households. Many were put to work planting and growing corn, tobacco, sugarcane and indigo. Slaves would usually be given their own piece of land to cultivate their own food, build housing and make their own necessities. Keeping with tradition, they rested and worshipped on Sundays.

When construction began on Fort Conde at the new Mobile site in 1723, the fort was built using slave labor. Twenty Black slaves and five White laborers built the eleven-acre fort using local bricks, stones and clay. The interior walls were built with local cedarwood. Its ruins still lie at the corner of Church and Royal Streets in downtown Mobile on the south side of Mardi Gras Park. These ruins are the oldest known documentation of slave labor along the Gulf Coast. Across from these ruins lies a replica Fort Conde, built in 1976 to celebrate the country's bicentennial. The fort, now called Colonial Fort Conde, was built at a two-fifths scale of the original, but its design is similar. During construction of the George Wallace Tunnel along Interstate 10 in the early 1970s, ruins of the old fort were dug up and reenergized efforts to reconstruct the fort at its former site, where it now sits along Royal Street in the Church Street East Historic District.

Mobilians of African descent can be credited with the origination of dishes like gumbo, jambalaya and Hoppin' John long before those dishes became household names in America. The dishes particularly can be credited to Mobile's Creole population. Creoles in Mobile are those of African, European or Native American descent. A Code Noir gave legal protection to the slaves in Mobile. Code Noir was originally issued by King Louis XIV in 1685 but recompiled by Bienville again in 1724. It declared that husbands, wives and children would not be separated from a sale. It was a form of slavery a little more humane than what it became in the antebellum era of the 1800s. The enslaved of early Mobile could also buy their own freedom and enjoy "all of the rights privileges inherit to our subjects born in our kingdom." Under this model of slavery, some of the former slaves would go on to be slaveholders themselves.

The French and Spanish culture of the 1700s was dominated by the Catholic Church and its traditions. The church's support of interracial marriage, universal education for all and their conversion approach, which did not prohibit race, grew the population and status of Creoles in Mobile. Many Creoles enjoyed a lot of the same freedoms as Europeans. If a Creole was enslaved by their White owner, they could be freed and even inherit land from the owner. They could serve in the military, purchase land and do business. They voted and lived in integrated neighborhoods. Some served as doctors, ship owners and merchants even up until the late 1800s. No other place in the South did people of color have as much dignity as the Creoles of Mobile.

Those freedoms that many people of color enjoyed slowly started to change once Alabama became a state in 1819. Men and women who had grown up in Mobile lived harmoniously for the most part of Mobile's first century. An invasion of White men, particularly from other parts of the country, viewed these free people of color as a threat to the practice of slavery. Reconstruction era laws of the 1860s gave Creoles a glimmer of hope to have their freedoms return but Jim Crow laws in the South and particularly Alabama in the early 1900s gave Creoles and no one of color the rights of voting, land ownership and business dealings they had once enjoyed.

Every culture and people throughout Mobile's history have had to work extremely hard just to survive but none more so than African Americans. Not far from the present-day Fort Conde sits Kazoola, a bar/eatery located along historic Dauphin Street. Inside, the tables are filled with patrons looking for a late-night libation or a Sunday brunch of chicken and waffles, grits, sausage, eggs, bacon and fried chicken. The walls inside are filled with the landmarks and sights of a community just five miles north of Mobile called Africatown. The most well-known resident of Africatown was a man named Cudjo Lewis. Born Olueale Kassola from the Yoruba people in the region of Benin in West Africa. Kassola grew up and at the age of fourteen began to hunt with spears, shoot arrows and defend his town. In April 1860, the king of Dahomey invaded the town and took the people there as prisoners. They were sent to the coast and placed in a slave pen, also known as a barracoon, waiting to be sold and shipped across the Atlantic Ocean. Hundreds of men, women and children were kidnapped from their homes, brought to this barracoon and awaited their fate.

Meanwhile, in Mobile, on the eve of Civil War, a wealthy businessman named Timothy Meaher heard reports that the king of Dahomey was actively involved in the slave trade from the wars of local West African tribes. Meaher made a bet for $100,000 (upward of $1 million in today's dollars) that he could smuggle slaves back to the United States without getting caught, despite the abolition of the international slave trade by Congress in 1808. To Meaher, the federal law meant nothing. Meaher hired a man named William Foster to captain the ship. Foster loaded the schooner, *Clotilda*, with local pine lumber to disguise itself as a lumber boat. Food and drink on board the *Clotilda* consisted of 125 barrels of water, 25 barrels of rice, 30 barrels of beef, 40 barrels of pork, 3 barrels of sugar, 25 barrels of flour, 4 barrels of bread, 4 barrels of molasses and 80 barrels of rum used for trading with the slave dealers. These provisions were to last the 12-man crew the entire four-month duration of the round trip and 110 passengers for eight weeks of travel across the Atlantic. After five weeks of travel, the crew arrived on the shores of Dahomey. When Foster arrived in Dahomey, 110 people boarded on the eighty-six-foot schooner *Clotilda* in exchange for $9,000 in gold.

The *Clotilda* began its voyage back to the states with 110 African prisoners on board. Words cannot justly describe the putrid conditions the people on board endured. The people on board were naked and stuffed into the bottom of the ship's hull with very little ventilation to cleanse the odor of human feces under the warm summer sun. Everyone on board suffered from hunger and thirst, with just enough provisions to stay alive. Water was mixed with vinegar to help fend off disease. One of the 110 on board was Kassola, who later described the journey to Zora Neale Hurston: "I so skeered on de sea! De water, you unnerstand me, it makes so much noise! It growl lak de thousand beasts in de bush. De wind got so much voice on de water. Oh Lor'!"

Foster and Meaher came up with a plan to disguise the *Clotilda* as a boat in distress and had it towed into Mobile Bay in the middle of the night to conceal the ship's cargo. Foster met with Meaher just north of Mobile, where the people on board were divided up between Meaher, Foster and Meaher's two brothers; thirty-four others were sold to landowners throughout the state of Alabama. Meaher instructed Foster to burn the ship and evidence of the crime he committed. The *Clotilda* has lain at the bottom of the muddy Mobile River since. In 2019, the hull of the *Clotilda* was found by a local journalist, Ben Raines. Since the exploration, worldwide attention has been brought to the Mobile River and the hopeful resurgence of the Africatown community.

Kassola was given to Timothy Meaher's brother James, from whom he received his new name, Cudjo. Cudjo worked for James Meaher on a steamship and lived under Meaher's house during the Civil War. During the war, slaves ate bread, cornmeal, molasses and small rations of beef and pork. African dishes they longingly remembered were pineapples and palm oil stews. Women made coffee from burnt rice, wheat or corn and sweetened it with molasses. Slaves were allowed their own gardens, which provided vegetables like greens, turnips and collards. Orchards supplied peaches, apples and cantaloupe. Peanuts were a primary source of nourishment for slaves. Peanuts were easy to produce, rich in protein, and were easily harvested, stored and prepared. They could be eaten raw, boiled, roasted or placed in soups and sweets.

News of the Union victory made its way to Cudjo and survivors of the *Clotilda*. After a short celebration, they realized that, while free, they had no

A bust of Cudjo "Kazoola" Lewis lies outside the Union Missionary Baptist Church in Africatown. Lewis survived the voyage of the *Clotilda* from Africa to Mobile in 1860. *Author's collection, 2021.*

home of their own. In 1865, Cudjo took the last name Lewis. By 1880, he had married a woman named Abile, who had also been on board the *Clotilda* and the two began a family.

The men and women who had come here on board the *Clotilda* always longed for their native country. They pleaded to return back to Dahomey and worked in hopes of making enough money to return. Eventually, they realized that vision of returning to Africa was not feasible, so their next plan was to ask Timothy Meaher for land; he was, after all, responsible for their captivity to this new land where they had been brought. Meaher dismissed their requests but instead made a deal that the Africans would work for him for $1 a day until they had enough money to buy the land. Cudjo and others purchased two-acre plots of land from Meaher for $100.

African Town, as it was called at the time, was formed. African Town was a self-sustaining community of descendants who maintained their African traditions and spoke their native language. They formed their own school, church and self-government. The men worked in sawmills and on the railroad. Women wove baskets and planted gardens. The women walked to the local lumber mills and into Mobile with the baskets on their head, where they sold their produce: corn, sweet potatoes, okra and black-eyed peas. In addition to fruits like pears, plums, blackberries and peaches. they grew fig and pecan trees. Years later, one family started a business that cooked rice and peas; they baked corn bread, made stews of chicken and fish and sold them to the local lumber mills, where Black and White workers alike bought their home-made meals.

Cudjo Lewis outlived his wife, Abile (known as Celia throughout the community), and all of their six children. He was placed on disability in 1902, when he was injured in a train accident. In the late 1920s, author Zora Neale Hurston made several visits to see Cudjo for a book she was attempting to write on former slaves. That book, *Barracoon*, wouldn't be published until almost eighty years later. Written in Cudjo's native dialect, it is a must-read or listen. Cudjo was a respected elder in the community, and word began to spread around the country that Cudjo was the oldest living former slave in the United States. Reporters frequented Cudjo's home looking for interviews and stories. Cudjo died on July 26, 1935, and is buried in a graveyard next to his wife, children, friends and family, some of whom made the trek from Africa on board the *Clotilda* with Cudjo.

Today, thousands of cars drive by a bust of Cudjo Lewis on their way to pristine white beaches of the Gulf Coast on the land formerly owned by Cudjo, Meaher and the citizens of Africatown. That bust is located outside of

Kazoola owner Marc Jackson informs students about the history of slavery in Mobile and the Africatown community from the walls of his restaurant. *Author's collection, 2019.*

the Union Missionary Baptist Church. Driving by at fifty-five miles per hour, you would barely notice the bust of Cudjo, much less any other significant landmark from the Africatown community. That busy stretch of highway, Bay Bridge Road, is one of only three roads that cross the Mobile River from Mobile to neighboring Baldwin County, where millions of people visit each year. That road, however, has been a sense of contention among community members who have seen highways, bridges, paper mills and pollution fill the land and waters over the decades where Africatown once thrived in the mid-twentieth century. The highway literally and figuratively split the community in half, and residents say it hasn't been the same since.

The future of Africatown is hopeful. The discovery of the *Clotilda* has reinvigorated tourism opportunities that surround the vessel and African American history from the last slave ship the enter U.S. soil. The Clotilda Descendants Association is a thriving group that has given significant attention to the Africatown community and their story—a story of survival, endurance, and perseverance.

Kazoola, nestled on Dauphin Street in downtown Mobile, is not just another restaurant. Opened in 2016 by Marc Jackson, a native son of Africatown who grew up in a humble six-room single-family household, it's a testament to his unwavering commitment to his roots and his community. Leaving behind a lucrative banking career, Marc ventured into creating a space that not only serves soul-soothing dishes like oxtails, red beans and rice and chicken wings but also kindles a unique cultural exchange.

But Kazoola is more than just a place to savor exceptional soul food. It is a venue that stands as a beacon of change and transformation. From hosting health and wellness seminars and HBCU fundraisers to business forums and small business pop-ups, Kazoola has become a cultural hub. Its reputation has drawn U.S. senators, renowned actor Samuel L. Jackson, a bevy of musicians, TV personalities and hall of fame athletes.

The interior of Kazoola serves as a living museum, adorned with photographs capturing the legacy of Cudjo Lewis, a survivor of the *Clotilda*, the last known slave ship to arrive in the United States. Among the pictures, one can see Cudjo in his old age, a pipe hanging from his mouth, sitting outside his self-built wood-frame home. Another picture bears the image of the Union Missionary Baptist Church, which he helped build with his bare hands, a testament to Cudjo's resilience and determination. A bust of Cudjo now stands outside that church, a silent witness to the history of a people.

In Kazoola, patrons of all races converge for a Sunday brunch or a Friday night cocktail at the bar. However, for the descendants of Africatown,

Kazoola is more than a gastronomic attraction; it's a platform to tell the story of their ancestors. They are the only group of African Americans in the United States who can trace their lineage with absolute certainty—knowing exactly where they came from, who their ancestors were, how much was paid for them, who brought them here, the exact date of their arrival and where they landed. Today, these descendants are likely seen at Kazoola, eating, drinking, dancing or singing, keeping the legacy of their ancestors alive and vibrant.

6

CRACKING THE SHELL

THE A&M PEANUT SHOP AND CIVIL WAR LEGACIES IN MOBILE

The story of antebellum Mobile is a tale of growth, prosperity and, ultimately, suffering. In 1820, the city was a modest town with a population of 1,500. But by 1860, it had grown into the fourth-largest city in the South with a population of almost 30,000. The city's economy was booming, thanks in large part to the cotton industry, which made Mobile the second-largest exporter of cotton in the region.

But with the election of Abraham Lincoln in 1860 and the ensuing political unrest over slavery and states' rights, the country became increasingly divided. Southern states began voting to secede, and the Confederate States of America was formed in 1861. Meanwhile, in Mobile, most sympathized with the Confederacy but there was also a large contingent of the population from the North, with many men coming from states like Pennsylvania, New York and Connecticut to work in the cotton industry. Strong ties to the North and a strong population of foreign-born citizens made Mobile not as staunch secessionist as others throughout the South. Lincoln's election had caused what most Mobilians believed was a trade imbalance, with more exports coming out than imports coming in. Northern businessmen handled most of the marketing of cotton flowing through the city, which was destined for Northern or European textile mills. A majority of Mobile's imports came from New York City. Mobilians hoped a new nation would end the colonial relationship to the North and spur urban growth.

Union general Winfield Scott devised a plan to starve the South by implementing a blockade of all Southern ports. The food supply in the

South collapsed under this plan. Urban cities like Mobile relied heavily on local grocers, bakers and butchers, who saw their supply of food dwindle down to the minimum. Shortly into the war, after the fall of New Orleans in 1862, Mobile became the only major port along the Gulf Coast that could supply food and other supplies to the Southern states, but the Union blockade of Mobile Bay made it difficult for ships to pass through. As a result, middle- and lower-class Mobilians suffered greatly from material and food shortages. Even household essentials like ribbons, needle and buttons were hard to come by. This kind of inflation had never been seen before, and even staples like flour and sugar saw an astronomical rise in prices. Mobilians were frustrated and upset, particularly middle- and lower-class women, who saw their loved ones dying on the battlefield while plantation owners, mostly exempt from fighting, continued to grow profitable crops like cotton instead of food.

Soldiers, on the other hand, had to pay five dollars for a dinner of bakers' bread and butter, while coffeehouses charged one dollar per cup with an occasional "ironclad pie" thrown in. Despite their government-issued rations of corn bread and sorghum, soldiers in Mobile enjoyed luxurious living due to the abundance of seafood. Oysters, crab, shrimp and fish were available every month of the year, and the coast along the Gulf and along Mobile Bay was one vast oyster bed. It was said you could run your hand on the bottom floor of Mobile Bay and dig out oysters. Suffice it to say, oysters in Mobile Bay were extremely plentiful at the time. Two forts and breastworks made entirely of oyster shells were reported to be a half mile in length. For the Union soldiers, the white sandy beaches of the Gulf Coast proved to be a unique feature of this area. The wildlife inland, along with alligators and dolphins along the coast, were a novelty. The soldiers swam in the waters, bathed and enjoyed the abundance of shellfish for their diet. General Thomas K. Smith and Colonel Lucas Hubbard wrote in their diary that their diet consisted of oysters and bread throughout their time on Dauphin Island.

Other starving soldiers were reduced to a diet of hardtack, pork and peanuts. Peanuts at the time were a food only reduced to the lower class or slaves. "Goober peas" became a source of good nourishment to hungry men during the Civil War. Goobers were easily carried from camp to camp; they could be roasted, boiled or eaten anywhere, and they could also be used in pies and coffee without spoiling. Following the war, the popularity of peanuts soared. No longer was the legume considered a low-class necessity; it was a versatile and nutritious food that could be enjoyed by people of all classes and backgrounds. Peanut butter, in particular, became a beloved staple in many households and a popular ingredient in a variety of recipes, from sandwiches to cookies and beyond. Additionally, the peanut industry boomed as farmers began to recognize the crop's potential and began to cultivate it on a larger scale. Overall, the war played a significant role in elevating the peanut's status and cementing its place in the culinary landscape of the United States and beyond.

Today, on a walk down Dauphin Street in Mobile in the block between Conception and Joachim, the smell of fresh roasted peanuts fills the air. The A&M Peanut Shop is an icon in Mobile's food scene, founded in 1947 as a Planters peanut chain outlet; these stores could be found in downtown areas throughout the country. In 1949, Alfred Gibson was transferred by Planters to run the store, and by 1963 he had purchased the store from Planters, when they decided to sell the franchise. He opened the A&M Peanut Shop, named after himself and his wife, Mary. The smell of peanuts in the air on the sidewalk of Dauphin Street comes from a roaster that dates back to the late 1800s. It still roasts the peanuts daily and wafts that aroma throughout town, making it hard to keep walking by without stopping. The roaster was originally a wood-fired roaster; it has since been converted to natural gas, which has extended its life into its third century of operation in Mobile. The peanuts come from Fidler Farms in Silverhill, Alabama, which is located across Mobile Bay in neighboring Baldwin County. The A&M Peanut Shop sells approximately three hundred pounds of fresh peanuts on an average day but sells hundreds more during Mardi Gras or nights when a concert is in town down the street at the Saenger Theatre.

The A&M Peanut Shop looks much like it did in 1947, shelves full of peanuts of every kind, Creole, blanche and redskin peanuts. Homemade candies like the peanut clusters, chocolate cashews and coconut haystacks line the counter along with jellybeans, popcorn and candy corn. On the sidewalk outside of the store, several times each week a local jazz band called the Dauphin Street Stompers rehearses their songs for upcoming shows while hungry patrons stand in line, drawn in from the smell of roasted peanuts as they walk through the peanut dust on the sidewalk out front. People of all backgrounds and ages stand in line waiting, sometimes even celebrities. Comedian Mike Epps was in town for a show in 2015 at the Mobile Civic Center when he noticed the jazz band playing outside of the A&M Peanut Shop. He danced along to the tunes while notifying his social media following with the video and a message for them, "Me and my new band." The smell of peanuts and the sound of southern-style jazz

Harvest and Hardship

The glass cases of peanuts, pecans, cashews and more inside the A&M Peanut Shop. *Nicky Mendenhall, 2021.*

just go perfectly together. This is a day in the life on Dauphin Street in Mobile, Alabama.

On September 4, 1863, hundreds of men and women gathered in the Spring Hill community outside of Mobile and marched until they reached the primary business district of Dauphin Street, the same location where the A&M Peanut Shop sits today. They were carrying signs that proclaimed, "Bread and Peace" and "Bread or Blood." Armed with knives, hatchets, hammers and brooms, they broke windows of local stores and looted food and clothing. The Mobile Cadets were dispatched to quiet the angry women, but even they could not contain the rioters. The *New York Times* reported, "The Cadets were defeated and taught to fly in their first action, and the mob ruled the hour." The rioters declared that if some means were not quickly devised to relieve their suffering or stop the war, they would burn the city. The Confederate general dispatched local troops to solve the conflict, but they did nothing. They were sympathetic to their women—wives and sisters. This caught the attention of Mobile's mayor, Robert Slough, and the provost marshal, who promised relief to the angry rioters by asking wealthy Mobilians to donate funds for food and clothes. They later formed relief committees, which helped the locals with their needs and prevented any future bread riots from occurring. The story of the bread riots of Mobile is a story of desperation and suffering but also one of resilience and community. Despite the challenges they faced, Mobilians banded together to demand change and find ways to help one another even in the midst of this tumultuous time in our history.

The Civil War had a significant impact on food availability in Mobile, as it did in most places in the South. As the war progressed, blockades made it challenging to get everyday supplies, and luxuries were the first to disappear. Mobilians quickly noticed the absence of items like shoes, clothing, cigars from Havana and staples like sugar and coffee. However, before the war, Mobilians planted a lot of corn, which proved to be a valuable resource. Farmers in Alabama and Mississippi began switching from cotton to corn production as the war progressed, and Alabama became a major bacon producer during the conflict. In exchange for cotton coming down the rivers, Mobile's merchants sent pork, corn, flour and whiskey to the planters and farmers of the interior. During the war, Mobilians relied on blockade running to get essential supplies. If they didn't get caught, they could make a profit of over 500 percent. Captains realized they could profit from citizens' shopping lists, and people would pay top dollar for essentials. Even ice was hard to come by in humid, hot, south Alabama. Before the war, it had come from New England on large frozen blocks from Walden Pond that was sawed off from the previous winter, carted to the local wharves in Massachusetts and shipped south on schooners covered in burlap to prevent them from melting before arriving in Mobile.

Not all was terrible for the southern soldiers in Mobile: theaters were open, and a five-dollar cover charge could give the men entertainment to enjoy the evening. The men took strolls along Shell Road, Government Street or along Dauphin Street, where bands would play in Bienville Square twice each week. A group of officers reportedly made their residence at the Battle House, where they indulged in a regimen consisting of whiskey, music and female companionship. Preaching in the streets occurred daily, and religious worship helped some of the men cope with being away from their families.

The Union navy was unable to get any closer than twelve miles from Mobile due to natural defensive advantages, such as swamp marshland from the north and a large sandbar in the bay. As a result, the Confederacy had almost four years to fortify the city, with Fort Morgan and Fort Gaines defending the mouth of Mobile Bay into the Gulf of Mexico. Torpedoes in the shallow bay and landmines made it impossible to steer a ship from the

Gulf of Mexico into Mobile Bay. Swampy lands gave a natural fortification along the western limits of the city and made it almost impossible to attack Mobile from the west. Thus, Mobile was the last major city to be attacked during the war. General Joseph Johnson even declared Mobile the strongest fortified city in the South.

War tactics had changed by the time of the siege of Mobile. No longer were generals charging a direct assault. This more resembled the battles of World War I. Torpedoes and sea mines were more effective in Mobile Bay than anywhere else in the war, making the Union navy timid. The most infamous Civil War skirmish in Mobile's history occurred on August 5, 1864, the Battle of Mobile Bay. During the engagement, Union admiral David Farragut proclaimed his famous words, "Damn the torpedoes, full speed ahead!" The Union victory there gave the Union control of only the bay, not the city, but control of the waters is what they sought. Mobile was the final seaport along the Gulf of Mexico to surrender control to the Union. The Mobile Campaign to control the city itself wasn't until March 1865. The Union decided to come in from the East and take the city. Battles at Spanish Fort and Blakeley were decisive Union victories. They outnumbered the Confederates eighteen thousand to four thousand. The Confederates saw no hope and evacuated Mobile on April 10, 1865, the same day Lee was surrendering to Grant in Appomattox, Virginia,

Depiction of the Battle of Mobile Bay. *Library of Congress.*

The A&M Peanut Shop has been a staple for generations in downtown Mobile. *Nicky Mendenhall, 2021.*

effectively ending the war. It would, however, take decades for the city of Mobile to recover financially from the war.

Almost a century later, Alfred Gibson's daughter Deborah was born, almost inside the Peanut Shop, when Mary went into labor one day. Deborah has been a staple at the store ever since. She worked here as a young girl and ran the store after her father's passing. Even though she sold the A&M Peanut Shop to a local attorney in 2018, she still works periodically throughout the week. She comes in to continue making the homemade confections found in the store and greets her regular customers who have been coming to the A&M Peanut Shop for generations. It's a rite of passage for parents in Mobile to continue the tradition of taking young children to the A&M Peanut Shop, not only for the candy, peanuts and chocolate but also for a bag of roasted peanuts to feed to squirrels in nearby Bienville Square located less than one block away. Hundreds of healthy squirrels race through the park at a time waiting for a handful of A&M's peanuts to hit the ground so they can enjoy.

A Mardi Gras mystic society formed out of the squirrels' obsession for A&M's peanuts. The Mystic Squirrels of Bienville, or Mystic SOBs, were formed out of the Mobile Arts Council as a Joe Cain Day parading group. They are a foot marching group that you'll find at the "tail" end of the Joe Cain Day procession. Members are dressed as squirrels, with squirrel masks and tails, while throwing handmade nut necklaces made from pecans and acorns glued together on a hemp string. It makes for one of the most unique throws that you can catch the entire Mardi Gras season. They also throw small brown bags of roasted peanuts courtesy of the A&M Peanut Shop.

A throw of peanuts away from the parade route, you'll find the A&M Peanut Shop on Dauphin Street. Deborah can take pride in the fact that her family's business will continue on for many more years, an iconic institution of Mobile's food scene.

PART III
THE MELTING POT

IMMIGRANT INFLUENCES AND CULINARY PROGRESS IN TWENTIETH-CENTURY MOBILE

7

THE CHANGING TABLE

THE DEW DROP INN AND THE CULINARY SCENE OF MOBILE IN THE 1900s

At the dawn of the twentieth century, Mobile found itself on an upward trajectory after years of decline following the Civil War. With a robust economy and thriving commerce, the city was experiencing a period of growth and prosperity. Railroad lines spawned throughout downtown with warehouses lining the river and wharves. Timber had replaced cotton as Mobile's economic powerhouse. More than thirty sawmills operated in the Mobile area. Barges and ships lined the newly dredged Mobile River, now with a depth of twenty-three feet allowing larger ships to safely transport cargo from Mobile to the Gulf of Mexico without the threat of their boats plunging the bottom of Mobile Bay.

Throughout the majority of the twentieth century, the downtown Mobile waterfront was lined with warehouses situated alongside the banana docks, which played an essential role in the city's economy for nearly one hundred years. Companies such as the Mobile Fruit and Trading Company, Snyder Banana Company and United Fruit Company generated substantial wealth through their banana trade activities with Central and South America, connecting Mobile to these vibrant markets.

Sam Zemurray, one of the most renowned figures in Mobile's banana industry, made a fortune in this trade. Born on a modest farm in Russia, Zemurray immigrated to the United States in 1891 and eventually settled in Selma, Alabama, by 1893. It was in Selma that the young Sam encountered his first banana. At that time, bananas were regarded as rare and exotic fruit. Although Mobile had been importing bananas since 1820, the trade flourished in the 1880s and 1890s due to the establishment of American plantations in Central and South America. By the dawn of the twentieth century, nearly half a million bunches of bananas were arriving at the port of Mobile, making it the country's third-largest banana importer.

During that era, bananas were manually unloaded by African American laborers who lined up to remove each batch from steamships and transfer them onto conveyor belts. There, the bananas would undergo a thorough inspection before being weighed and marked for their final destination. Workers then loaded the approved batches onto refrigerated rail cars, filling them to capacity before closing the doors. The trains departed for various destinations across the Midwest, such as Chicago and St. Louis, as well as southeastern cities like Birmingham and Montgomery. When one train was full, another took its place. If a batch of bananas failed inspection, indicating they were likely to spoil before reaching their destination, they were set aside and sold at a discount to local shop owners and peddlers at day's end. Bananas deemed "ripes" were discarded altogether and left to decay in the sweltering Alabama heat.

Sam Zemurray identified a unique opportunity with the ripened bananas that had been overlooked by others. With $150 in his pocket, the eighteen-year-old entrepreneur purchased as many ripened bananas as possible to fill a boxcar headed for Selma. His plan involved selling as many ripened bananas as he could to merchants and peddlers along the route. It was a race against time. Despite encountering delays on his initial run, Zemurray managed to make a $35 profit for six days of work before returning to Mobile. For his subsequent trip, he persuaded the telegraph operator to notify towns ahead of the fresh bananas available for sale; in exchange, the operator received a commission on sales. The strategy proved successful. In 1899, Sam sold 20,000 bananas, and within a few years, he had sold 500,000, earning the nickname Sam "The Banana Man" Zemurray.

Sam Zemurray eventually relocated from Mobile to New Orleans, where he went on to purchase his own steamships, cargo and plantations in Honduras. Under the Cuyamel Fruit Company, he imported bananas directly to Mobile. Later, Zemurray became president of the United Fruit Company, which was famous for its Great White Fleet. By 1946, United Fruit employed 83,000 workers and owned over 116,000 acres dedicated to banana cultivation. Although Sam "The Banana Man" Zemurray eventually left Mobile, his experiences and lessons learned in the Port City contributed to one of the most remarkable entrepreneurial success stories in the history of the United States.

Men like Sam "Banana Man" Zemurray made a fortune selling unwanted bananas or "ripes" to local farmers and producers. *Library of Congress.*

Meanwhile, back in town, breathtaking hotels like the Bienville Hotel, the Cawthon Hotel and the newly rebuilt Battle House Hotel—which reopened in 1908 after a devasting fire—opened during the first decade of the twentieth century. Just around the corner from the Battle House Hotel was the newly constructed Van Antwerp Building. Towering over the commercial buildings of downtown, the eleven-story skyscraper was the first of its kind in Mobile: a reinforced concrete skyscraper, designed by architect George B. Rogers, that would house Garet Van Antwerp's drugstore filled the bottom floor. The top floors, however, were not filled. Mobilians were not particularly excited to be so high in the sky until Rogers moved his office to the top floor. That finally convinced Mobilians that it was safe.

Spanning fifty-three feet in length, an elegant white marble soda fountain graced the interior that, upon the building's completion, was acclaimed as the "finest in the United States." The Van Antwerp family's own herd of dairy cows provided the milk used to create ice cream and frozen buttermilk at the seat of this main feature inside the Van Antwerp Building. Just three blocks down Dauphin Street from the Van Antwerp Building was a busy port. Timber, lumber, coal, cotton and bananas along with other goods that made Mobilians' lives easier were brought in by the boatload. One block south of the Van Antwerp Building sat Klosky's.

Simon Klosky was a native of Austria and came to Mobile in 1857. During the War Between the States, Klosky enlisted in the Confederate navy, and he eventually became a prisoner of war. After the war, he returned to Mobile, where he opened an oyster stand inside the Arcade saloon. By 1881, he had opened the Delmonico restaurant on St. Michael Street. A decade later, he opened Klosky's at Royal and Conti Streets. It was here where Klosky became one of the most famous restaurateurs of the early twentieth century. He even operated a hotel there on Conti Street under the same name. Oysters, green turtle soup, soft shell crabs and gumbo were talked about all over town.

One block east of Klosky's restaurant at Conti and St. Emanuel Streets, a new dining concept was the talk of the town upon its opening in 1920. Morisson's Cafeteria opened in the bottom floor of the German Relief Hall. John Arthur Morisson became familiar with cafeteria-style restaurants from his travels but saw that no one provided the level of service at these cafeterias that were usually found in restaurants. At Morisson's Cafeteria, white-jacketed waiters served customers by carrying their tray to their table in exchange for a small gratuity. This novel concept proved to be an immediate success. Within a week, Morisson and his initial staff of forty served lunch and supper to 1,000 customers per day. The initial menu consisted of seventy-three menu items but eventually grew to over one hundred; chopped steak, fried chicken, dozens of fresh vegetables and desserts like custard pie were served to Mobilians for decades. It wasn't long before a second location in Mobile was opened along with locations in Pensacola, Jacksonville and Montgomery. With the average meal costing not much more than ten cents, this inexpensive but satisfying way of dining carried Morisson's through the Great Depression of the 1930s without missing a beat. Throughout the Southeast, 700,000 customers a year were eating at Morisson's Cafeterias. Home-style meals became a staple of restaurants throughout the South. As of this writing, the last remaining Morisson's Cafeteria is still operating in the town where it began, Mobile. The Springdale Plaza location was open in 1967 as the 154th Morisson's location. Dining trends and company restructures through the years shuttered all but the last remaining Morisson's Cafeteria. A testament to James Arthur Morisson and his vision for a concept that he wasn't entirely sure would work lasted over one hundred years in the Port City.

In 1924, another restaurant opened not long after Morisson's Cafeteria on Ann Street near Government, serving an innovative culinary delight at the time, the hot dog. George Widney operated a sandwich shop at the location before moving to Old Shell Road in 1930, where the Dew Drop Inn has been an iconic place to dine in Mobile ever since. The current location in the wooden chalet-style building dates to 1937. The dining room dates to a renovation done by then owner Jimmy Edgar in 1967. Shortly after, Edgar sold the Dew Drop Inn to George Hamlin, who was advised not to change anything in the restaurant. "Don't change nothing." "You don't change the dining room, or the help." "You don't change the hot dog or nothin'." So, the Hamlin family hasn't. The Dew Drop Inn Hot Dog is known widely as one of Mobile's signature dishes. Served with homemade chili, sauerkraut, mustard, ketchup and pickle paired with fries or onion rings, there's no more Mobile dish than that.

The Dew Drop has a loyal following of regulars who dine on much more than hot dogs. Gumbo, fried oysters and fried shrimp along with sides like mashed potatoes, fried okra and turnip greens grace the menu. Hamburgers and cheeseburgers are also served daily. Mobile's famous son Jimmy Buffett said that his "burger lust was formulated" from many meals growing up at the Dew Drop Inn. Jimmy has become somewhat of a cheeseburger aficionado since recording his hit single "Cheeseburger in Paradise."

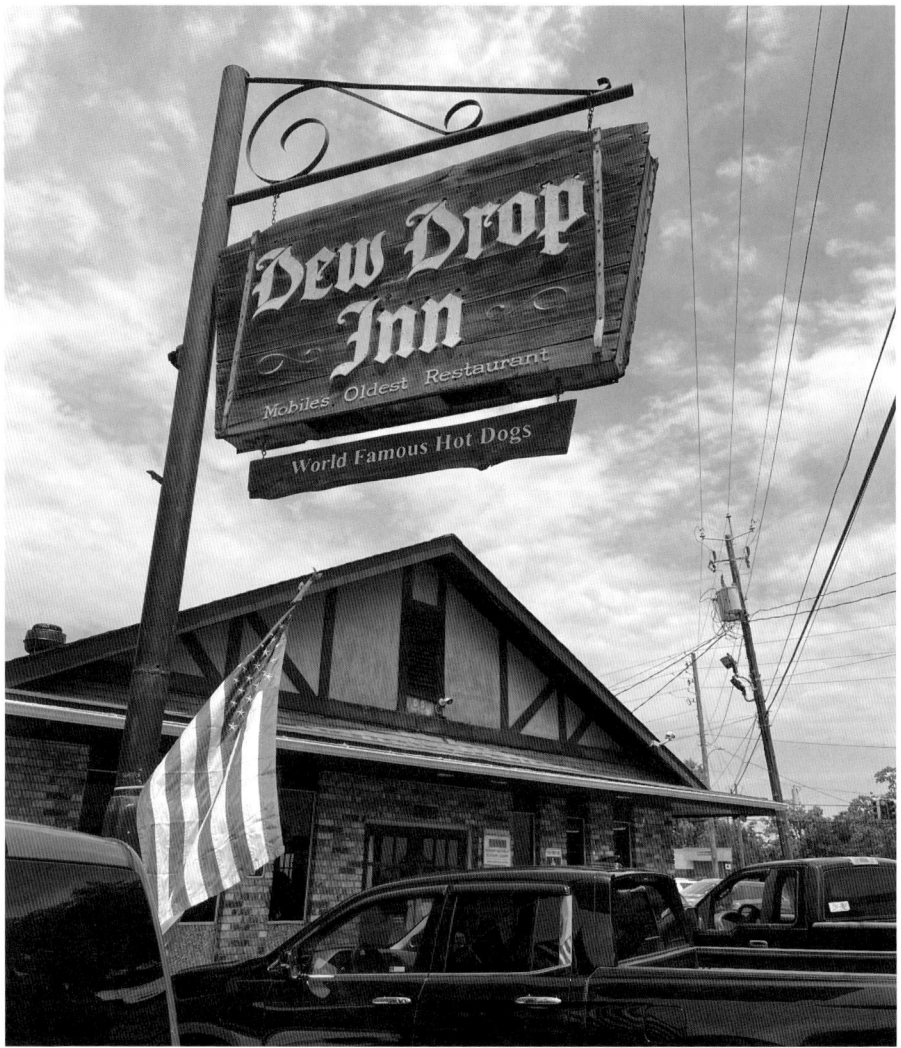

The Dew Drop Inn is an iconic institution in Mobile, Alabama. *Author's collection, 2023.*

Whether you crave the Dew Drop Hot Dog that put the Dew Drop Inn on the map or the wide variety of other dishes, this historic eatery has something to satisfy every palate. Its legacy has left an indelible mark on Mobile's food scene, transcending generations and earning the admiration of locals and our future celebrities alike. The unwavering commitment to preserving the authentic flavors and atmosphere of the Dew Drop Inn has not only cemented its status as an iconic Mobile institution but also ensured that the cherished memories and dining experiences of patrons like Jimmy Buffett continue to be shared and savored by future generations on Old Shell Road.

The period between World War I and World War II saw modest population growth in Mobile. However, tourism emerged as a burgeoning sector, significantly contributing to the city's economic expansion. The automobile transformed Mobile's historic streets, not always for the better. Government Street was lined with beautiful mansions at the start of the twentieth century, but many were bulldozed within decades. U.S. Highway 90 was one of the original numbered highways planned to connect Americans in 1926. U.S. 90 ran from Jacksonville, Florida, to Van Horn, Texas, where it connected with U.S. 80 west to San Diego, California. In 1929, Sam Lackland convinced the Mobile Junior Chamber of Commerce (Jaycees) to sell and plant azalea bushes along Mobile's throughfares to increase tourism in the spring months. Tourists flocked to see the Azalea Trail, which spanned fifteen miles of residential and commercial streets of Mobile. The Jaycees decided to establish an Azalea Trail Court made up of fifty high school girls who would represent and serve as official hostesses of the city of Mobile. The Azalea Trail Maids continue to this day, showcasing the best of Mobile County's most talented young women. Sam Lackland's vision for tourism was fulfilled, but not without the help of his next-door neighbor, Walter Bellingrath. Lackland convinced Bellingrath to open the first azalea garden along the Azalea Trail in 1929. Countless numbers of cars would drive past the Bellingrath home each spring in admiration.

In 1903, Walter Bellingrath had moved to Mobile to start an exciting new entrepreneurial adventure in a start-up business at the time called the Coca-Cola Bottling Company. Bellingrath began in Mobile with one mule, one wagon and a hand and foot bottling machine that churned out a few cases of Coca Cola each hour. By 1948, the Mobile Plant was included in the list of the fourteen-largest Coca-Cola plants in the United States. Walter Bellingrath amassed a fortune selling soft drinks in Mobile. In 1918, heeding his doctor's recommendation to alleviate the stress of his professional life, Bellingrath purchased a small fish camp just south of Mobile as a peaceful retreat from the demands of business. His wife, Bessie, loved to garden, and she was inspired by the beautiful estate gardens found in Europe to transform their fishing camp into a pristine showcase of flowers and beauty. For years, Bessie worked on the gardens. Finally in 1932, Walter Bellingrath put an ad in the *Mobile Register* inviting all to come see the finished gardens. Almost five thousand people came out the next day to see the azaleas, camellias and more. In 1934, Bellingrath Gardens officially opened to the public year-round with a charge of one-dollar admission to enter, and by 1939, Bellingrath Gardens would see fifty-eight thousand people per year.

Coca-Cola and soft drinks not only played a pivotal role in Walter Bellingrath's entrepreneurial journey but also indirectly contributed to the growth of tourism in Mobile. The fortune that Bellingrath amassed from his successful Coca-Cola venture enabled him to create the breathtaking Bellingrath Gardens, which eventually became a cornerstone of the city's tourist attractions. To this day, Bellingrath Gardens continues to draw visitors from all over the world, eager to admire the exquisite floral displays.

Departing from the Bellingrath property by boat, travel half a mile down Fowl River until you approach the point where the river merges with Mobile Bay. At this juncture, you'll find the Dauphin Island Parkway overpass. Head north for approximately one and a half miles, and you'll arrive at an intersection called Bayley's Corner. Be cautious not to drive too quickly, as you might easily overlook one of Mobile's most significant culinary landmarks: Bayley's Restaurant.

Bill Bayley, a towering figure originally hailing from Texas, embodied the adage that "everything is bigger in Texas." Bayley not only boasted an imposing physical presence but also made a grand impact with the innovative and delectable West Indies Salad, which he claimed to have invented. West Indies Salad originated from Bayley's time as a Merchant Marine, where he traveled the world serving lobster salad and cucumber salad throughout the Caribbean. Today, the perfect West Indies Salad requires fresh Gulf lump crab meat, diced sweet onions, cider vinegar and Wesson vegetable oil topped with salt and pepper.

After serving as a Merchant Marine, Bayley relocated to Mobile, where he met his future wife, Ethel. Together, they opened a modest one-room restaurant on Dauphin Island Parkway in 1947. Rapidly evolving into a culinary sensation, the establishment eventually expanded to accommodate up to five hundred patrons, all drawn to the renowned appetizer West Indies Salad. Bill Bayley also pioneered the concept of serving fried crab claws. Though the claws were previously considered waste by chefs, Bayley had the ingenious idea to fry them and offer them as a dish in his restaurant. This inventive approach led to the creation of another iconic appetizer, akin to the West Indies Salad, which would gain widespread popularity in seafood restaurants across the Southeast, all originating from Bayley's Restaurant in Mobile.

Top: The renowned West Indies Salad, a culinary masterpiece by Bill Bayley, originated in his namesake restaurant, Bayley's, just south of Mobile. *Author's collection, 2020.*

Bottom: Fried crab claws from Bayley's Restaurant. Bill Bayley was the first to fry crab claws and serve them. *Author's collection, 2020.*

Following World War II, Mobile saw an incredible population boom not seen since the antebellum period. People moved here to work in the shipbuilding industry and to assist in the war time effort. Brookley Field was an aircraft maintenance facility for the U.S. Army and at its height employed more than seventeen thousand people. During this time, food trends in the United States began to shift, with frozen foods and convenient processed meals gaining popularity. In Mobile, diners and homestyle restaurants continued to thrive. Along the Mobile River, meals derived from recreational hunting and fishing—featuring deer, bear, wild turkey and various shellfish—never went out of fashion. A unique phenomenon called a jubilee occurs on the shores of Mobile Bay; it is found in only two places worldwide. While jubilees typically take place on Mobile Bay's Eastern Shore, they can also happen on the western shore under the right conditions. These events are most common in the summer months when the weather is just right, with winds coming from the east and allowing the large bluffs of the eastern shore to create calm, smooth waters. This calmness causes the fresh water from northern rivers and the salt water from the south to mix, creating a challenge for the oxygen-dependent bottom-dwelling sea creatures in Mobile Bay. Desperate for oxygen, they approach the shore, giving rise to the phenomenon known as a jubilee. In response, people rush to the bay, nets in hand, to catch the bountiful shrimp, flounder, crab, stingrays and other seafood. In the past, bells would ring to signal a jubilee; nowadays, people simply text or call one another to spread the word.

The causeway, situated just east of Mobile and connecting the city to Baldwin County, saw a rise in popularity as numerous restaurants emerged along the shoreline. Since its opening in 1957, the Bluegill Restaurant has remained a favorite spot for locals. Over the years, a multitude of establishments such as Roussos, John Word's Captain's Table, Palmer's, Pier 4 and several others have dotted the bay, offering visitors an enticing combination of fresh seafood and exceptional service.

Although Mobile's restaurants remained segregated until the passage of the Civil Rights Act in 1965, African American entrepreneurs in the city forged their own paths in restaurant ownership. Lamar Powell was one such trailblazer, owning seven restaurants and clubs in the Mobile area. His most famous establishment was the Flame Restaurant and Social Club, located in Mobile's "Avenue" district. Since its opening in 1941, the Flame became renowned for its signature hot sausage sandwich and fried fish sandwich. For four decades, the Flame remained open 365 days a year, not only providing an exceptional dining experience but also contributing to Mobile's civil rights movement during the 1960s and '70s.

Family-owned restaurants such as the Best Grill were a staple in the "Avenue" part of Mobile during segregation. Founders Oliver Henderson Sr. and his wife, Artherine Henderson, originally established the family-run restaurant in 1948 at 1056 Davis Avenue and Monday Street. Alongside six of their ten children, the Hendersons worked together daily to uphold the restaurant's esteemed reputation as the "best grill" in Mobile. Oliver managed the restaurant during the day, while Artherine took charge in the evenings. Their daughters, Yvonne, Myrtis and Paulette, were waitresses. Sons Vincent and Harold were responsible for maintaining the exterior of the building. They diligently swept and washed the sidewalks in front of the restaurant and neighboring businesses every day. In 1954, Marvin, their oldest son, returned from military service in Korea and took on the role of day manager at the restaurant. Notable patrons of the Best Grill included Jackie Robinson, Fats Domino, Thurgood Marshall, Roy Campanella, B.B. King, and Ray Charles.

George Moore, a man who witnessed Mobile's transformation throughout the twentieth century, spent his childhood on Warren Street until 1948. Growing up, he tended to chickens, fig trees and plum trees while also playing baseball and football with the neighborhood boys. His first job was at Constantine's on Royal Street, where he washed pots for fourteen dollars a week. Despite some pots being as heavy as his 120-pound frame, Moore was dedicated to his work. Additionally, he worked as a food runner at the Battle House Hotel, as African American men were only allowed to be food runners and banquet waiters at the time. During the bustling 1950s, Mobile flourished with department stores such as Gayfers, Hammel's and Sears and a thriving shipbuilding and stevedore industry. In 1968, Moore began working at the newly opened Malaga Inn and later joined the Riverview Hotel in 1983 as a manager. He continued to work there until 2007, when the newly opened Battle House Hotel invited him back. Today, the hotel's gift shop bears George Moore's name, welcoming visitors from around the world. It's a testament to how far both Moore and Mobile have come—from a time of segregation to a bustling city with world-class establishments like the Trellis Room and a renowned spa.

The latter part of the twentieth century saw a westward expansion in Mobile. The newly built Interstate 65 brought businesses like shopping malls, hospitals and car dealerships west. The 1,200-acre University of South Alabama opened in 1964, and neighborhoods continued to flourish in

West Mobile. To the east, the completion of the George Wallace Tunnel and Interstate 10 Bayway made travel to Mobile Bay's Eastern Shore easier than ever before. Mobilians flooded to these suburbs in droves, leaving a once thriving downtown anything but. With that, Mobile saw many of its most popular places to eat open in these neighborhoods.

The delightful flavor of Creole Praline ice cream at Cammie's Old Dutch Ice Cream Shoppe. *Author's collection, 2020.*

Midtown Mobile has its fair share of iconic spots. In 1969, Edwin Widemire established Widemire's Old Dutch Ice Cream Shoppe at the corner of Old Shell and Florida Street, using his father's recipes. The ice cream shop thrived and continues to do so under the ownership of Cammie Wayne. Cammie started working at Widemire's when she was just sixteen and eventually purchased the store in 1998, renaming it Cammie's Old Dutch Ice Cream Shoppe. By 2011, she had started crafting her own ice cream flavors in-store. A trip to Mobile is now considered incomplete without a visit to Cammie's Old Dutch, which features forty-seven flavors, including the crowd-pleasing pecan praline. Remarkably, the store's appearance has remained virtually unchanged since its opening in 1969. Located just a cone's throw away from Cammie's Old Dutch, Butch Cassidy's Café has been a local favorite since its opening in 1993. Founded by Roy Seewer, the "Soon to Be Famous Butch Burger" has already made its mark, selling hundreds of burgers each day and earning a reputation as one of the best burgers in Mobile.

Also in Midtown Mobile exists a distinct area known as the Loop, named after the streetcar routes in the early twentieth century that would travel west along Government Street before looping back downtown. This unique neighborhood is home to several legendary restaurants that made a lasting impact during the twentieth century. The Tiny Diny on Halls Mill Road catered to Mobilians for six decades, offering a diner-style experience with home-cooked breakfast, lunch and desserts, such as Mrs. Trudy's Lemon Ice Box Pie. The Pillars and Korbets were also renowned fine-dining establishments located in the Loop.

Situated in West Mobile, Dick Russell's BBQ has been a fixture in the city since 1954. While many patrons are drawn to the establishment for its barbecue, steaks and seafood, locals particularly rave about the daily made from scratch biscuits and breakfast offerings. Another cherished favorite in Mobile, dating back to its opening in 1996, is Big Time Diner. This establishment is well known for its blue-plate specials and meat-and-three dishes, but its classic Mobile creations like seafood gumbo and green beans almondine should not be overlooked.

Under the revitalizing guidance of Mayor Mike Dow in the 1990s, a vision for a rejuvenated downtown Mobile emerged through Dow's "String of Pearls" initiative, which encompassed a convention center, a minor-league baseball team and numerous downtown building renovations. This forward-thinking plan set the stage for Mobile to make a significant stride into the twenty-first century, leading to transformative changes in the city's restaurant and food scene.

8

A SWEET LEGACY

GREEK IMMIGRANTS AND THE LEGACY OF THREE GEORGES

Restaurants owned by Greek immigrants have been instrumental in shaping the culinary landscape of Mobile, Alabama. Since the early days of the city's founding, these immigrants have brought their distinct flavors and traditions from Greece, contributing to a rich and diverse dining experience that has become a defining aspect of the city's restaurant scene.

Throughout much of Mobile's history, restaurants owned by Greek immigrants have been synonymous with fine dining in the city. In the late nineteenth and early twentieth centuries, Greek immigrants arrived in Mobile from major cities in the North with little to no money. Most of them arrived with not much more than the clothes on their body. Most spoke very little to no English and, usually upon their arrival, took any job they were offered. Despite their difficult circumstances, these immigrants proved to be exceptionally hardworking and entrepreneurial people. Many opened fruit stands, sold fresh fish door to door, made candy and treats and even ventured into the realm of fine dining. Regardless of their chosen line of work, the common theme was a commitment to hard work and determination.

In fact, the Greek community quickly established itself as a driving force in Mobile's culinary scene, with Greek-owned restaurants quickly gaining a reputation for exceptional cuisine and hospitality. The Greeks' success in the food and beverage industry can be attributed to their strong work ethic, as well as their commitment to quality and hospitality. The impact that the Greek community made to the city's culinary scene is still felt and cherished to this day in Mobile at places like Three Georges Candy Shop.

The Melting Pot

Open in downtown Mobile since 1917, Three Georges Candy is one of the oldest businesses in town. Three Greek immigrants all named George—George Pappolamporous, George Pope and George Spero—opened the business as entrepreneurs looking to make their way in Mobile during World War I. The three Georges originally had a debate among themselves about what exactly they wanted to serve inside their store. Each had a different vision: one George envisioned a sandwich shop, another a soda fountain and the other a chocolate store. After their disputes and disagreements, eventually, their wives convinced them to serve all three. This plan worked perfectly and still does to this day inside the iconic building at 226 Dauphin Street. Trials have certainly come their way in over a century of business. A devasting fire in 1929 saw Pope and Spero leave the business with George Pappolamporous, who by this time was going by George Pappas and re-opened as George's Candy Shop. George Pappas Jr. took over the business following his father's death in 1937. George's Candy Shop moved to several different locations throughout the downtown area before settling in 1972 at the circa 1866 building where Three Georges currently sits today. While things have certainly changed throughout the building and the surrounding downtown area since then, many things remain the same. The gigantic Greek marble slabs still cool the chocolate alongside the original mahogany cases, the candy cannisters, the marble countertops, the giant copper pot and, most importantly, the century-plus-old recipes.

In 1992, Scott Gonzalez purchased the family business from George Pappas Jr.'s widow, Euple, and became the new owner of Three Georges Candies. Euple passed down her knowledge and expertise in candy and chocolate making to Scott, who learned the art of candy making under her

The interior of the iconic Three George's located in downtown Mobile. *Stacy Cole, 2019.*

guidance. Even after selling the business to Scott, Euple remained at the store for many years, overseeing the kitchen and continuing to dip chocolate. Today, her presence is still felt in the store, as an antique sign reading "Euple's Kitchen" hangs above the copper pot on the wall.

Under Scott's ownership, Three Georges Candies has undergone a transformation, returning to its roots as a candy and lunch counter. Scott added new items to the menu, including traditional New Orleans-style muffulettas, hearty gumbo and delicious chicken salad. He also reintroduced the soda fountain, serving ice cream and milkshakes just as in the early days of the store. The new Three George' Candies not only serves up sweet treats but also provides a cozy atmosphere, thanks to the use of mahogany wood from the former First National Bank Building in constructing the soda fountain and the barstools that were once used at the former Woolworth lunch counter located across the street. The original Three Georges logo was also brought back and is proudly displayed, a testament to the store's rich history and tradition. Euple would be proud of the store today, as it continues to thrive and honor the legacy of the Pappas family.

The year Gonzalez purchased the candy shop from Euple Pappas, a native Mobilian, Winston Groom was in the process of having his book *Forrest Gump* become a movie that would become a Hollywood sensation and one of the greatest movies of all time. Winston Groom grew up frequenting George's Candy Shop as most children do growing up in Mobile. Groom made sure that Three Georges was included in the festivities that surrounded the movie. He even commissioned the candy shop to make chocolate-covered shrimp on one occasion for the film stars. Winston Groom even told Scott during one of their conversations that he was thinking of Three Georges when he penned one of the most famous movie quotes of all time, "Life is like a box of chocolates, you never know what you're gonna get." The now famous line is a source of pride for the small candy store in Mobile thanks to Winston Groom's love of the store and its chocolate.

A decade before the three Georges opened their downtown store, Antonios Markopoulos arrived in Mobile after emigrating from Greece to Chicago. Markopoulos changed his name to Jason Malbis and together with his friend William Papageorge traveled the country in search of a place to start a Greek community. The men settled on 120 acres they purchased for five dollars per acre just across Mobile Bay in rural Baldwin County, where they cleared land for farming and growing crops. Farming thrived on the land. Malbis continued to maintain relationships with merchants and business owners in Chicago. Using those relationships, his crops from Baldwin County would be sent all over the country. The plantation included an ice plant, a canning factory, a nursery and an electric power plant. In 1927, Malbis had five miles of road laid to connect to the newly built causeway that allowed vehicles to cross Mobile Bay into Mobile quickly for the first time. Now that travel to Mobile was simple, Malbis assisted the Metropolitan Restaurant in Mobile when its owner became ill. The restaurant thrived with Malbis's assistance, but he soon realized the gap in quality bread for his customers. Malbis Bakery opened in 1925 and a year later opened in a beautiful new facility at Broad and South Carolina Streets with all of the newest technology in bread baking equipment. Malbis even opened a restaurant on-site. Malbis Bakery sold baked goods all throughout the Southeast with a fleet of over fifty trucks. At capacity, the bakery could make up to 100,000 pounds of bread per day and an additional 85,000 pounds of crackers and cookies with a workforce of four hundred. Other bakeries in Mobile would originate from the massive workforce through the years at the Malbis Bakery.

Malbis died of colon cancer in 1942 during a visit to his homeland of Greece. Knowing his own illness, he left instructions for a Greek Orthodox church to be built on his land at the Malbis Plantation. In 1965, the magnificent church was built using funds from the sale of Malbis Bakery in Mobile. Jason Malbis's remains lie interred in the crypt of the Malbis Memorial Church. The church, one of the most historic churches in south Alabama, that Jason Malbis had built on his land still stands as a tribute to his generosity and vision. Though the Malbis Plantation has undergone significant changes over the years, with four-lane highways and bustling shopping centers now occupying the land, Malbis's legacy continues to inspire and influence the food and business communities in Mobile and Baldwin County.

The most legendary Greek restaurateur from the city Mobile also, like Malbis, made his way to Mobile via Chicago. Constantine Panayiotou worked as a dishwasher in restaurants and hotels throughout the Chicago area before moving to Mobile in 1924. Constantine first opened a hole-in-the-wall restaurant on St. Francis Street across from the Battle House Hotel. It was there he got his start in the restaurant business specializing in ham and tomato sandwiches for fifteen cents and coffee for five cents. It was also there at his first location that Panayiotou learned about customer service. In those early days, to make things easier for his customers when times were tough, Gus instituted an honor system where they could come in and enjoy a meal, sign their name in a book and pay their tab on payday. Panayiotou

A marker depicting the former location of Constantine's, one of the most popular restaurants in Mobile's history. *Author's collection, 2022.*

never had any issues with this system, as he knew and trusted his customers. However, one day a stranger caught on to the plan and took advantage of it. The man came into the café, ate two ham-and-tomato sandwiches, signed the book and disappeared without paying. Panayiotou was disappointed but didn't let this ruin his trust in his community. Years went by, and Panayiotou had all but forgotten about the sandwich thief. One day, a well-dressed man walked into the café and ordered a sandwich with coffee. When it was time to pay, the man handed Panayiotou a ten-dollar bill and said, "Keep the change. I've owed you money since the day I signed the book and walked out without paying for my meal." Panayiotou was surprised but grateful for the man's honesty. He forgave him and even joked that he may have come back just for the ham-and-tomato sandwiches.

In July 1934, Constantine's Restaurant reopened, this time across from the Battle House Hotel on Royal Street. It was here that Panayiotou became the iconic restaurateur at "Mobile's Finest Restaurant." The restaurant was known around the South for dishes like scamp almondine or its menu of fresh seafood like red snapper, trout and Florida lobster. The meats ranged from lamb chops and chicken to filet mignon. Fresh vegetables, made-from-scratch salad dressings and desserts were sold twenty-four hours a day at Constantine's. At its peak, Constantine's served over two thousand meals each day. The restaurant made the move from downtown to west Mobile in 1964 following a fire. Constantine Panayiotou died in 1970, leaving his son George in charge for the remainder of its existence. Constantine's closed in 1984, but its lasting impact on Mobile's food scene is still felt today. George Panayiotou would later serve Constantine's recipes and spins on dishes at the Cooper family of restaurants in Mobile, including Felix's Fish Camp, Ruth's Chris Steak House and the Bluegill Restaurant.

Greek-owned restaurants in Mobile dominated the food scene throughout the twentieth century. In 1949, George and Katie Kordomenos opened Korbet's on Airport Boulevard in the area of town known as the Loop. Their son Nick and his wife, Ethel, operated the restaurant until 1995. Korbet's was a favorite in Mobile for special occasions, business meetings or family gatherings for many years.

Pete Zitsos operated the first cafeteria at the newly opened University of South Alabama campus starting in the mid-1960s. Pete also operated the Dauphin Room on the bottom floor of the Van Antwerp Building before opening his namesake restaurant in 1979. Zitso's Cafeteria was a cafeteria-style restaurant located in the basement of the First National Bank Building until it closed in 2008. Zitso's served workers inside the bank along with others in the downtown community with breakfast and lunch. Pete's Greek-style dishes like Greek snapper and chicken were not to be missed along with southern favorites like red beans and rice, gumbo and hashbrown casserole served for lunch, while dishes like catfish and grits or a scrambled egg sandwich were served at breakfast.

George Roussos emigrated from Greece to Mobile, where he worked with his uncles at Harry's Restaurant on Beauregard Street. George ran a couple of other restaurants in town before finally opening Roussos Restaurant on the Causeway in 1974. On September 12, 1979, Hurricane Frederic made landfall on the Alabama Gulf Coast as a strong Category 3 hurricane. Roussos was completely destroyed during the hurricane, leaving nothing intact but the Roussos sign out front. Two years later, Roussos reopened on South Royal Street in Mobile, where it operated for many years. It was there that Roussos became an institution in Mobile for its seafood and Greek dishes. The seafood gumbo, the stuffed flounder, Greek salad, baked oysters and "chicken George" were mainstays on the menu at Roussos. Roussos dishes continue to appear to this day at various weddings, Mardi Gras balls and class reunions around town through his daughter Georgia, who owns and operates Georgia Roussos Catering.

In 1962, a group of parishioners from the Greek Annunciation Church in Mobile decided to host a one-night event called Greek Night. This event would celebrate Greek culture by sharing that culture with the Mobile community through food, dance and music. Greek Night eventually formed into Greek Fest, now a weekend-long celebration of food like gyros, lamb shank, Greek fries and Greek salads. Pastries like baklava, kourabiedes and almond cookies. You will find Greek dancing, Greek music and imported Greek beer. Tours of the historic church, lectures and exhibits are also given during the weekend festival. Greek Fest has evolved from a modest one-night event to a cherished weekend-long cultural extravaganza that continues to bring the vibrant spirit of Greece to the Mobile community.

At 226 Dauphin Street, Three Georges Candy serves as a testament to the enduring legacy of the Greek immigrant community in Mobile, Alabama. As one of the city's oldest and most cherished businesses, the candy shop stands as a proud symbol of the determination, entrepreneurial spirit and strong work ethic that defined the early Greek settlers who ventured to Mobile in search of opportunity. Their unwavering commitment to quality, hospitality and the sharing of their rich cultural heritage has left an indelible mark on the city's culinary landscape. As each new generation continues to savor the sweet treats at Three Georges, they also celebrate the vibrant history and enduring influence of the Greek community that has shaped Mobile into the diverse and flavorful city it is today.

9

FROM HAVANA TO MOBILE

PROHIBITION TALES AND CUBAN CONNECTIONS AT LAS FLORIDITAS

Mobile has always had a proclivity for alcohol and spirits. As Mobile was founded as a French town in the early eighteenth century, alcohol was central to the living experience, especially at its former location at 27 Mile Bluff. Life was hard for the new Mobilians. Famine and disease were always rampant, as was the threat of death. Life was also celebrated by the religious men. The first Fat Tuesday in Mobile's history was likely celebrated by men of Catholic faith drinking beer in a tavern prior to the Lenten season of 1703. Wine was made by the Frenchmen, bottled and traded in those early days. It was, of course, drunk by the men in Mobile. The University of South Alabama Archaeology Department has excavated many wine bottles at the old site, which was appropriate for a port city in the 1700s. Rum was brought to Mobile from many of the Caribbean islands, like Cuba. At one point in Mobile's first century of existence, a native Choctaw chief frustratingly declared that "rum pours in upon our nation like a Great Sea from Mobile."

Trade with the Natives or West Indies islands like Cuba continued for more than a century. Mobile and Cuba have always had a strong bond. Only 629 miles separate the two Gulf ports. One of our founding fathers, D'Iberville, established and built trade routes with Havana, Cuba. In 1706, on one of his supply runs to Cuba, D'Iberville contracted yellow fever; he died there and is buried in the Church of San Cristobal. His younger brother and cofounder of Mobile Bienville was left to govern the colony in Mobile. To this day, a statue of D'Iberville is found on the waterfront of the

A statue of d'Iberville stands at Cooper Riverside Park in downtown Mobile. An identical statue stands 629 miles away in Havana, Cuba. *Author's collection, 2022.*

Mobile River along Cooper Riverside Park. His eyes gaze in the direction of Havana, Cuba, where an identical statue of him is located on the Cuban seafront, staring right back to the banks of the Mobile River. This symbolizes the relationship between Mobile and Havana that was formed in 1993 by former Mobile mayor Mike Dow. It was the first agreement between a U.S. city and a Cuban city to become Sister Cities.

While travel to Cuba today is limited for Mobilians, you can still experience the unique culture at Mobile's Cuban-themed speakeasy Las Floriditas. Las Floriditas was first opened in 2020 by owner Bob Baumhower, who is an aficionado of Cuban history and culture. The speakeasy is located inside the former bank vault of the RSA Trustmark Bank Building. The vault is still there and very much a part of the décor along with the former deposit boxes, which pair well in the dim-lit speakeasy. When there's not live music playing, guests enjoy the sounds of Cuban-style music like son cubano, salsa or timba. Las Floriditas is not easy to find, as any good speakeasy should be. It's also not easy to enter, as it requires a password to gain access—again, as any good speakeasy should. Las Floriditas is a tribute to Ernest Hemingway, whose favorite bar in Havana was called El Floridita. Once you find the entrance to Las Floriditas inside the basement of the RSA Trustmark Bank Building, you'll see Hemingway there hoisting a massive tuna. You'll also find the doorkeeper sitting in his chair—that's Mr. Roosevelt Patterson. You'll be greeted by Roosevelt in his fedora hat and Cubavera shirt, but he will only let you enter unless you know the password. The daily password can be found in italics on Las Floriditas' social media pages. It might look something like this: "I drink to make other people more INTERESTING." —Ernest Hemingway. The word *interesting* will gain you access behind the bookshelf just for that evening. Before his time as the doorkeeper at Las Floriditas, Roosevelt was a star football player: member of the Mobile Sports Hall of Fame; a football national champion from Vigor High School just outside of Mobile, in Prichard, Alabama; a national champion for the 1992 Alabama Crimson Tide football team; and fifth-round NFL draft pick of the Los Angeles Raiders. Baumhower often spoke of his plans to open a Cuban speakeasy in the bank vault below where his outstanding fine-dining restaurant Dauphin's is located on the thirty-fourth floor of the RSA Trustmark Bank Building. Roosevelt heard word that he would be looking for a doorkeeper once it opened and jokingly remarked to call him once it did. Baumhower didn't take the joke and later called Patterson to tell him he wanted him to be the doorkeeper. The two former NFL players have worked together ever since. Roosevelt has become one of the most recognizable faces in Mobile.

Once inside Las Floriditas, the menu is full of authentic Cuban-style dishes, such as appetizers like Ceviche Havana topped with fresh Gulf shrimp, fried plantain chips and raw oysters. Entrees include an authentic Cuban sandwich, which is as good as you'll find on the northern Gulf Coast, a barbacoa sandwich and the Hemingway Bowl. The Hemingway Bowl is

Roosevelt Patterson sits to greet guests upon their entrance to Las Floriditas, a Cuban-themed speakeasy in Mobile, Alabama. *Author's collection, 2021.*

named for the famous author and served with barbacoa, black beans, rice, avocado and lime. The desserts at Las Floriditas are some of the best in Mobile. Guava flan is a classic Cuban guava-flavored custard topped with caramel and a flan sauce. The Trio of Mousse includes chocolate Cuban coffee, hibiscus and Key lime. The coconut tres leches is a signature of the dessert menu. This classic Latin American dish is a layered sponge cake with cream and toasted coconut flakes. Most guests never leave Las Floriditas without a libation—it is speakeasy after all. Signature cocktails include the Las Floriditas cocktail—white rum, mixed with fresh Key lime juice, maraschino liqueur and turbinado sugar—and the Cuba Libre, a classic rum and Coke served with Mexican Coca-Cola. Daquiris, mojitos, piña coladas, wine and even authentic Cuban coffee are offered on the extensive drink menu. Las Floriditas is a place that would make Hemingway proud to be found in Mobile.

Mobile has always had a bent for places along the Mobile River like Las Floriditas. Bars and saloons that catered to working-class sailors, rivermen and stevedores lined the riverfront during the early years of Mobile's American history. On an 1850s visit to Mobile, John Oldmixon observed that every street corner seemed to boast a lively gathering spot. He described these places as featuring grand spaces complete with bars, a vast array of bottles on display and the ever-present sounds of Swiss organs or "hurdy-gurdies." In these establishments, crowds of people could always be found sipping drinks and enjoying the atmosphere. Today, the thought of waterfront dining or sipping on a cocktail overlooking the river is a sign of luxury due to the modern technologies and safe building codes that allow people an opportunity to enjoy food or drinks by the water. These establishments are typically upscale restaurants or trendy bars where patrons relax and enjoy scenic views while enjoying delicious food and drink. This is not the norm in Mobile's history. Most establishments closer to the river were often rowdy and disorderly places where seafarers and pirates would come to drink, gamble and fight. The lack of sanitation also meant also meant waterborne illnesses like cholera or typhoid were common. Women of the night would roam these bars looking for adventure or attention from men in the dark streets along the Port City.

While Mobilians have long enjoyed imported wines and Cuban rum to our shores, at the beginning of the twentieth century, Cubans were known to enjoy beer brewed right here in Mobile from one of the two breweries in town. The Bienville Brewery and the Mobile Brewering Company brewed from their respective breweries in downtown Mobile, and because of late-nineteenth-century advances in refrigeration methods, these breweries could ship beer made in Mobile all over the Southeast, to Central America and to Cuba. The breweries wouldn't survive Prohibition but still show Mobilians' love for beer long before the modern-day breweries arrived to help make the thriving brewery scene we have today.

Michael Krafft began the country's first secret mystic society from these bars along Dauphin Street in 1830 when he drunkenly stumbled into a hardware store and later proclaimed with his friends the start of the Cowbellion de Rakin society. Secret societies that parade in Mobile and in New Orleans during Mardi Gras both trace their roots back to a libatious night along Mobile's waterfront corridor. The Cowbellion de Rakin society would eventually host elegant balls where menus reflected their penchant for champagne. The Cowbellion de Rakin society later gave way to other mystic societies; the Strikers, Order of Myths and the Infant Mystics all continue the tradition of celebrating the Carnival season with good food and drink, primarily drink. That tradition continues to this day, where meetings occur throughout the year and glasses are raised formally. More informally are the day or night of the parades, when libations begin early in the morning at breakfast or brunch, continue until parade time and throughout the parade, then last well into the evening at the ball or even the next day for some.

Mobilians never affectionately adopted the temperance movement that occurred throughout the South toward the end of the nineteenth century. The only temperance on alcohol that Mobilians would accept would be during the Lenten season. Breweries and saloons filled the town at that time. When the State of Alabama enacted a prohibition law in 1907 that banned the sale of alcohol, a local delegation from Mobile threatened succession from the state. Bank of Mobile president N.J. McDermott wired this message to legislators in Montgomery: "Unless anti-prohibitionist win, please give notice that Mobile is prepared to secede from the State of Alabama." That law lasted only two years. The Alabama legislature passed another law in 1915, the "bone dry" law, five years before Congress passed the Eighteenth Amendment imposing a federal prohibition of alcohol. The idea of Prohibition was to reduce crime and foster a moral society. However, reality was quite the opposite. Prohibition instead gave rise to more crime and an entire underground economy of bootlegging, rumrunning and moonshiners.

Mobile's location on the northern Gulf Coast made it a hotbed for illegal activity during Prohibition. Rumrunning and the conspiracies that surrounded it were big business for many along the Gulf of Mexico, where liquor was pouring in through its shores and ports. Smugglers anchored their boats at "Rum Row," located miles offshore and well outside the jurisdiction of federal authorities. On Rum Row, the rumrunners exchanged orders or booze for cash payments. Over 500,000 cases of liquor were being shipped each day from Havana, Cuba, alone. Europe sent liquor to the islands in the Caribbean, namely places like Cuba; that liquor would, in turn, end up in the United States through elaborate schemes. For Mobile, its location along Mobile Bay, the Mobile River and many of its inlets and bayous provided opportunity for smugglers to distribute to the Port City.

Despite the enactment of Prohibition laws locally and eventually nationwide with the Eighteenth Amendment in 1920, most residents in Mobile were unconcerned, especially when authorities, for the most part, were not stern at enforcing the law. The lack of enforcement locally was due to corruption in local government, while lack of federal enforcement was due to the fact that the number of federal agents just could not enforce such a large amount of illicit activity. Lines were blurred throughout the entirety of Prohibition. Consumption of alcohol was never outlawed, but the sale, production and transport were considered illegal under the law. In fact, public consumption continued the entire time. In 1926, for example, 874 people were arrested for public drunkenness in Mobile.

The Catholic Church has long held a more lenient view toward alcohol consumption compared to some Protestant denominations, which often advocated for total abstinence. Moderate alcohol consumption was generally considered acceptable within the Catholic community, with wine being an essential part of the sacrament of the Eucharist. This more permissive attitude toward alcohol, combined with the strong Catholic presence in Mobile, played a role in the relaxed attitude toward alcohol temperance. Mardi Gras, Mobile's annual celebration held in the days leading up to the Catholic observance of Lent, also played a large role in shaping the city's attitude toward alcohol. Mobile's celebrations during the 1920s afforded revelers the opportunity to flaunt the alcohol ban in the public. Alcohol was no longer openly served at mystic balls in the ballrooms of places like the Battle House Hotel; instead, guests were given a key upon entry that would give them access to a room where the alcohol could be found.

The southern portion of Alabama was issued only six federal agents by the government to patrol the area. Prohibition agents were underfunded and ill-equipped to prevent smuggling in Mobile. Agents did discover liquor sealed aboard ships that were docked in Mobile's dry docks. The *Saccaroppa* was one such steamship found to have hidden 30 cases of "high grade" liquor like champagne, scotch and cognac. The liquor was found in a sealed tank

A Cuba Libre inside Las Floriditas, Mobile's Cuban-themed speakeasy in downtown Mobile. *Author's collection, 2020.*

that only a mechanic could unseal because of the steel lid used to disguise it. While most illegal activity occurred on a small scale in the area, one raid made national news, all the way to the *New York Times*, when it involved some of the most prominent residents and politicians in the Mobile area. In November 1923, federal officials confiscated more than 10,000 quarts of liquor from warehouses and speakeasies, also known as "blind tigers." The feds rented every large truck in town to help confiscate the liquor to the federal building, where it took the authorities hours to unload the booze. Some 415 cases were confiscated from one address on Conception Street during the massive raid. The liquor was valued at over $100,000. In total, over seventy men were arrested and indicted. Once they were indicted, the list of names stunned the town. Mobile County sheriff Paul Cazalas, Mobile police chief Patrick O' Shaughnessy, state representative William Holcombe, a former sheriff, chairman of the local Democratic Party, a local bank president, attorneys and wealthy businessmen like Frank Boykin were all indicted. Hugo Black, who later served as a U.S. senator and Supreme Court justice, was the lead prosecutor of the case. Allegations were that the men operated a wholesale liquor business that reached not only the entire Gulf Coast region but all the way to Chicago as well. Monthly, at least one member of the ring would travel by boat into the Gulf, where rumrunners operated, and return to Mobile with hundreds of cases that originated from Cuba or elsewhere in the Caribbean. The cases were stored in warehouses and businesses in Mobile and shipped aboard a train to Chicago. Many of the barrels of liquor were labeled as turpentine to disguise the operation. The conspiracy was vast. The banks were in on it, law enforcement was paid to keep quiet and city officials were paid to ignore the organized liquor market in Mobile. It was a raid so enormous it led undercover investigator Izzy Epstein from New York to say that "he had never seen a city with so high a proportion of 'shinny joints.'" The same could be said one hundred years later in Mobile.

The legacy of Mobile's resistance to Prohibition lives on today as you stroll along Dauphin Street. The historic street is lined with restaurants, bars and venues offering "shinny joints" to thirsty Mobilians and visitors alike. Las Floriditas is one of the best places to eat and drink in the entire Southeast. You will need the password to enter this modern-day speakeasy, but you'll have no need to look over your shoulder these days, so sit back and relax to sounds of live music and sip on a daiquiri that would make Ernest Hemingway, Michael Krafft and Hugo Black proud.

PART IV
A NEW ERA OF EATS

MOBILE'S TWENTY-FIRST-CENTURY FOOD REVOLUTION

10

CARNIVAL CUISINE

KING CAKES, MOON PIES AND THE JOE CAIN CAFE

Mobile is certainly known for having a good time. The city's visitor and convention bureau even markets the city as "Born to Celebrate." While most of the United States experience the blues of winter following the Christmas season, in Mobile the party is just getting started. Hundreds of thousands of people arrive on the streets of Mobile each year to celebrate one thing: Mardi Gras. This celebration is the annual event that unites all people in the city. Now for out-of-towners, you need to know that Mardi Gras is technically not the season we are celebrating. Carnival is the season of revelry, parades, balls and parties between Twelfth Night and Fat Tuesday. The Twelfth Night is January 6, which celebrates the arrival of the three kings to Jesus's birth according to some historians and traditions. Mardi Gras is French for Fat Tuesday, the day before Ash Wednesday, when the Christian Lent period begins. Mardi Gras Day traditionally falls on the calendar exactly forty-six days before Easter Sunday. The day fluctuates every year because of the Easter holiday. Easter Sunday is always the Sunday after the first full moon following the first day of spring. Mardi Gras Day will never occur any earlier than February 3 and never any later than March 9.

Mardi Gras was celebrated in the New World for the first time on Tuesday, February 20, 1703, in Mobile at the former site of the town at 27 Mile Bluff. That first celebration centered heavily on food, drinking and dancing. Conditions were harsh for the men of the colony. Supplies like food, clothing and weapons from King Louis XIV were limited, as there were delays in shipping coming from France. After several years of searching the Gulf Coast for a suitable capital, the men could at last celebrate this reverent day with the food did they have. The early celebrations likely consisted of meals from vegetables, corn or sagamite—a Native American stew made from cornmeal and animal fat. Sagamite was served with beans and passed around in a bowl to share. The drink offerings consisted of beer, ale or wine. Recent excavations at 27 Mile Bluff by the University of South Alabama Archaeology Department have found many wine bottles on the site and even the location of a few taverns. The celebration in 1703 likely centered on men of Catholic faith drinking beer in a tavern the day before Ash Wednesday. Group singing and dancing with the Natives may have also been an appropriate celebration for the inaugural Mardi Gras celebration in the New World. These early celebrations were nothing like those we know today. Modern-day Mardi Gras in Mobile with secret societies, balls and elaborate parades wouldn't get its start here until over a century later.

Modern-day secret society parading in Mobile began in 1830 when the Cowbellion de Rakin society was formed. Michael Krafft, a young cotton broker who moved here from Pennsylvania, had a few drinks on Christmas night in 1830 and stumbled into a hardware store on Dauphin Streets. He ended up getting into some cowbells, rakes and gongs. He then recruited some of his friends to join him, and when he got the attention of his fellow citizens, they asked him, "What society is this?" The "Cowbellion de Rakin" society, he proclaimed! All of this chatter made the local papers, and word traveled quickly. A crowd of people showed back up on New Year's Eve to see whether the Cowbellions would return. Sure enough, Michael Krafft returned—this time with around forty of his friends. They paraded down the streets in costumes going door to door with loud music all the way to the mayor's house, where they serenaded him. A tradition was started. By 1840, the Cowbellion de Rakin society had evolved to revelers wearing masks on horseback, parading through the streets on horse-drawn floats presenting elaborate, theatrical themes such as "Heathen Gods & Goddesses" but always parading on New Year's Day.

In 1857, six members of the Cowbellion de Rakin society moved to New Orleans, where they started the Krewe of Comus, the first mystic parading society in New Orleans. They, however, paraded on Mardi Gras Day instead of New Year's Day. However, Carnival as we know it today with floats, throws, parades and revelry on Mardi Gras Day wouldn't begin in Mobile until 1868, when Joe Cain danced onto the scene.

A New Era of Eats

At the corner of Royal and St. Francis, inside the historic Battle House Hotel is a restaurant called Joe Cain Cafe. Joe Cain is our founder of modern-day Mardi Gras in Mobile. The story every child growing up in Mobile hears is that Joe Cain marched the Union-controlled streets of downtown Mobile dressed as a fictional Chickasaw Indian, Chief Slacabamorinico, on his coal wagon and lifted the spirits of war-beaten Mobilians, and that is how Mardi Gras in Mobile was reborn following the Civil War. Now that story might be slightly exaggerated to some degree, but there's no doubt Mardi Gras in Mobile would not be the same today if not for Joe Cain.

Born in 1832, Joseph Stillwell Cain Jr. from an early age was fascinated with mystic societies, especially the ones that paraded on New Year's Eve in Mobile. In 1866, a year after the Civil War was over, Joe was member of the Washington Fire Company No. 8. It was a well-respected fire company throughout the country. In 1867, Joe and Washington No. 8 were invited to the annual Firefighters Parade in New Orleans, which at the time was well attended and a big deal among the locals in the Crescent City. The firefighters parade also coincided with Mardi Gras that year, and Joe had so much fun that he was determined to bring that celebration back to Mobile with him. In 1868, Joe and his six sidekicks, called the Lost Cause Minstrels, mounted a dilapidated coal wagon and preceded the very first Order of Myths parade in Mobile. The band of mostly Confederate veterans serenaded the crowds that had formed with what was described later in the papers as "the most discordant music." The story of Joe Cain and his legacy on Mardi Gras can be debated, but what is not debated is that Joe Cain brought fun to Mardi Gras.

Parades up to that point were proper, portraying themes of literature, which gave them an elite status among the majority of people in the crowds at the time, who couldn't read or write. Joe Cain declared that Mardi Gras was going to be for all and, most importantly, *fun*. Mobilians celebrate Joe Cain Day in Mobile the Sunday before Mardi Gras Day, the day of the "people's parade"—signifying that Mardi Gras and Carnival are for all Mobilians to enjoy. You do not have to be a member of a secret society or Mardi Gras organization to parade on Joe Cain Day. All you need to do is show up ready to have a good time. Joe Cain Day has been a tradition in Mobile since 1967, when local historian Julian Rayford declared that Joe Cain was one of the most important figures in Mobile's history. In 1966, Rayford convinced the family of Joe Cain to disinter his body in Bayou La Batre, Alabama, and then convinced the City of Mobile to have him reburied in the Church Street Graveyard, which had been closed to the public since 1898, when it

A statue of Joe Cain dressed as Chief Slacabamarinoco at Mardi Gras Park in Mobile, Alabama. *Author's collection, 2020.*

became full. Rayford kicked off that inaugural Joe Cain Day dressed as Joe Cain's Indian character, Chief Slacabamorinico. In 1974, a mystic society known as Cain's Merry Widows began. This secret group of ladies mourns the death of Joe Cain by gathering around his grave for a time of lament. The women, dressed in all black and disguised by their veils, continually argue throughout the day about who Joe Cain loved the most. The ladies leave the Church Street Graveyard and make their way to Joe Cain's house on Augusta Street for a toast to Chief Slac. Finally, they ride in the Joe Cain procession on a black bus or limo through the parade route.

Inside the Joe Cain Cafe is a photograph of Joe Cain dressed as Chief Slacabamorinico in his plaid skirt, turkey-feathered headdress and deerskin belt, probably taken later in his life. At the café you'll get a glimpse of the real Joe Cain. You'll also taste some of the best pizza in Mobile from its coal-fired ovens. Many Mobilians enjoy the Joe Cain pizza while waiting for the parade to start; it is a white sauce–based pie topped with chicken, bacon and spinach. The menu largely revolves around sandwiches and wraps but also includes a chicken and sausage gumbo along with a red beans and rice with Alabama-made Conecuh sausage. The Joe Cain Cafe began when the historic Battle House Hotel was opened after renovation in 2007. The Battle House Hotel has been named the "Best Historic Hotel" in the United States by the Historic Hotels of America. Historically, the Battle House has been home to many balls, parties and luncheons for the different mystic societies.

Mobile native Jimmy Buffett recalled in his book *A Pirate Looks at Fifty* that as a child sitting on his father's shoulders outside the Battle House Hotel at the Order of Myths parade one Mardi Gras night he had his first encounter with Carnival's Folly and Death. Since the very first Order of Myth's parade in 1868, their emblem float has featured Folly chasing Death around a broken column—some say the broken column of life—beating Death with inflated pig bladders. Death looked the young Jimmy in the eye and laughed. Buffett then recalled "a crack that sounded like a gunshot." Folly had walloped Death on the backside with the traditional pig bladders. Jimmy recalled that moment he had his first encounter with Death but realized Folly was the only way to deal with it. While Death wins in the end, Folly for one day—Mardi Gras Day—wins. That lesson would with stay with Jimmy Buffett as a life philosophy and later in his successful music and entertainment career.

Today, parade-goers standing at the corner of Royal and St. Francis Streets are delighted by the sounds and smells of a parade. In addition to the Joe Cain Cafe, among others, concession food trailers line the parade

The Joe Cain Cafe located at the corner of Royal and St. Francis Streets in downtown Mobile. *Author's collection, 2021.*

route selling family favorites like chicken on a stick, funnel cakes, corn dogs, nachos, sausage dogs and cotton candy. Some families prefer to bring their own food to a parade: sandwiches, po-boys, ice chests full of cold sides like vegetables and shrimp salad and ice-cold beverages. Once the parade begins, all eyes are on the revelers riding the floats. In Mobile, the phrase "Throw me something, Mister!" almost always can be translated as "Throw me a Moon Pie!"

Moon Pies and Mobile are synonymous with each other. These marshmallow cookies are sandwiched between two flavored graham crackers, primarily chocolate or banana, but can come in a variety of flavors. Moon Pies are baked in Chattanooga, Tennessee, at the Chattanooga Bakery but have become the signature throw of Mardi Gras in Mobile since they started flying in the 1950s. Legend of the Moon Pie originated in the coal mines of Kentucky when one miner asked for a "snack as big as the moon"—a treat that fit in the miner's lunch pail but also filled the coal miners' stomach through the day of long, hard work in the mines. Sometime during the Great Depression, Moon Pies were paired with RC Cola and became the South's most iconic working man's lunch.

Mardi Gras parade throws go back as far as the 1860s, when young men threw fistfuls of flour from the floats onto spectators—usually, well-dressed men were the target. It wouldn't be until the 1940s that parade-goers began to raise their hands at the revelers riding in floats. This led to throws of candy, taffy and Cracker Jack. The City of Mobile banned Cracker Jack from being thrown in 1971 when men, women and children were getting injured by the sharp edges of the boxes. The Cracker Jack ban only increased demand for Moon Pies. After all, they are soft and cheap, and everybody in the South loves Moon Pies. More than nine hundred Moon Pies are thrown during each parade in Mobile, accounting for over four million that are purchased and thrown just during a single Carnival season. Now, ironically, boxes of Moon Pies are sometimes thrown, even to the displeasure of parade-goers and authorities, despite the fact that sharp corners were the reason the Moon Pie tradition began in the first place. Heavy, sharp cornered boxes of Moon Pies are sometimes thrown, so always keep your head up!

Moon Pies are a favorite throw during each and every Mardi Gras parade in Mobile, Alabama. *Library of Congress.*

Moon Pies and Mobile are so synonymous that the Port City is even home to the World's Largest Electronic Moon Pie. Located at the northeast corner on top of the RSA Trustmark Bank Building is a six-hundred-pound, 12-foot-tall electronic Moon Pie that drops 317 feet in one minute. The yearly tradition began on New Year's Eve 2008 when City Councilman Fred Richardson promoted the idea as a way to draw tourists and residents downtown to help increase revenue for hotels, restaurants and businesses in the area. The Moon Pie drops yearly to ring in another year in the Port City, but the giant "pie in the sky" is also dropped before each parade during the Carnival season. Moon Pies are not the only food thrown from floats by revelers during a Mardi Gras parade in Mobile. Groceries of all kinds have been popular throughout the twenty-first century. Peanut butter crackers, oatmeal cream pies, snack cakes, ramen noodles, ice cream sandwiches and even Conecuh sausage have been seen in addition to the beads, doubloons and other trinkets.

The signature food item of Mardi Gras, however, cannot be found thrown from a float. The king cake is a beloved staple of Mobile's festivities. A traditional king cake is a circular pastry made of a sweet, yeasted dough that is typically filled with cream cheese, cinnamon or fruit preserves and decorated with brightly colored icing and sugar in the colors of Mardi Gras: purple, gold and green. Mobile's official Mardi Gras colors, however, are just purple and gold. Purple represents justice and gold represents power. New Orleans adopted green, representing faith, in the 1880s, but Mobile did not. In Mobile, king cakes are often served with a plastic baby figurine on top. The host should place the baby inside the king cake, and the person who finds the baby in their slice is said to have good luck and must provide the next king cake for the group. A king cake can only be eaten between Twelfth Night and Fat Tuesday. In Mobile, we jokingly say you jeopardize Joe Cain Day with rain if you do not abide by these rules.

King cake is the signature food item during Carnival season in Mobile. *Author's collection, 2018.*

In ancient Europe, Twelfth Night was celebrated with a bread or pastry with a bean or coin placed inside. The one who found this piece was declared the "king" of the party as a way to mock the royals of the time. That king would choose his queen, be given a crown and rule the mischief of the party that evening. Eventually, a bean-sized baby Jesus was placed inside the treat to represent the discovery of the three kings who visited the birth of the Christ child. Today, bakers avoid the threat of a lawsuit by placing the plastic baby Jesus on top or to the side of king cakes. Nevertheless, king cakes are an important part of the Mardi Gras season in Mobile, as they are served at parties and other festive events throughout the season. It is a sweet and indulgent treat that brings people together and adds to the overall sense of joy and celebration during this special time of year.

Pollman's Bakery on Broad Street has been owned and operated by the Pollman family since 1918. Throughout the year, Pollman's is known for its po-boys, Cuban sandwiches, brownies, fruit cakes and chocolate dobash cakes, but when it's Carnival season in Mobile, Pollman's is the go-to place for king cakes. Pollman's is the original king cake dealer in the city of Mobile. It's been baking king cakes since 1959, the very first bakery in Mobile to do so. Each cake is baked fresh daily during the Carnival season, when the bakery is known to churn out over ten thousand each year.

Fred Pollman moved to Mobile from New Orleans in 1900 to assist his brother-in-law at Smith's Bakery. In 1918, Fred and his wife, Corinne, opened their own bakery at 708 South Warren Street in downtown Mobile. Later, the bakery moved to Royal and Congress Streets. Pollman's would deliver to stores and restaurants all throughout town via horse and wagon. In 1948, Pollman's moved to its current location at the corner of Broad and Virginia Streets. A decade later, Fred Pollman Jr., his brother Charles and sister Mary took over the operation. It was at this time the king cakes were born at Pollman's, and four generations later, the Pollmans are still baking bread, king cakes and other confections in Mobile. Fred Pollman III described to *Mobile Bay* magazine in 2013 the art of Pollman's king cakes:

> *We make them from scratch. First, we scale our flour, sugar and all our ingredients and mix the dough. We put it on the table and cut it up into the sizes that we need for large king cakes or small king cakes. Next, we round the dough up and let it relax. Then, we stretch it out to size and stuff it with our fillings, sugars and pecans. We fold, cut and braid it into the shape of a king cake. From start to finish it takes about two and a half hours to make up a batch.*

King cakes are such a hit in Mobile, there is even a King Cake Off hosted each year where bakers and vendors can hand out samples of the best king cakes and king cake–related treats to hungry guests. Dozens of bakers throughout town sell king cakes during the weeks leading up to Fat Tuesday, and all of them have Fred Pollman to thank for bringing this delicious treat to Mobile.

The importance of food and its relationship to Mardi Gras cannot be underestimated. Most organizations host a ball for their members. For parading organizations, balls usually occur following the parade. It's a celebration of dancing, eating and libations but also a time to celebrate the artistic side of Mobile's Mardi Gras. A tableaux tells the story of the theme for that year in theater and stories. Each organization has a king and queen introduced at the ball. Ball gowns and "costume de rigueur" is the strict formal dress code that is required at these mystic balls. Men are to wear a white tie and tails. Ladies are to wear a gown to the floor. This spectacle takes place for invited members only. Food at most balls consist of catered meals that are served buffet style. Some balls are more formal seated dinners. Guests may enjoy a variety of finger foods like chicken tenders, dips and meatballs. You will also find seafood like gumbo, West Indies Salad and shrimp served at balls.

King Felix III and his queen are the official monarchs selected by the Mobile Carnival Association each year to reign over the festivities for that particular year. Each year, on Lundi Gras, the Monday prior to Mardi Gras Day, the king's knights and the queen's ladies of the court gather at Cooper Riverside Park on the banks of the Mobile River at the foot of Government Street as King Felix III arrives from the fictitious Isle of Joy. He is also greeted by the mayor of Mobile with a key to the city, beginning King Felix's reign of misrule in the city until the stroke of midnight on Fat Tuesday. During this time, the Queen's Luncheon is held in spectacular fashion by the empress and her family for the ladies only. The Felix Luncheon is the gentlemen's turn to celebrate. David Cooper Sr. reigned as King Felix III in 1971. Since then, his contribution to Mardi Gras and the food scene of Mobile has been huge. Cooper, a businessman, fell into the restaurant business when his favorite restaurant in Mobile, Ruth's Chris Steak House, was going out of business in 1997. Cooper drove to New Orleans to convince owner Ruth Fertel to not close the struggling Mobile location. She insisted he purchase the franchise, and after some thought, David Cooper was now in the restaurant business. Ruth's Chris in Mobile is not your ordinary steakhouse chain. Cooper added Mobile classics like West Indies Salad to the menu but also added the Chrissy cocktail. The Chrissy is an ice cream cocktail served at Ruth's Chris Steak House in Mobile but also found at many luncheons and balls throughout the Carnival season. Cooper would go on to open Felix's Fish Camp and take ownership of the iconic Bluegill Restaurant, both located on the beautiful Mobile Bay waterfront. Felix's Fish Camp, named in honor of King Felix III himself, opened in 2002 with an attention to customer service and hospitality that Cooper had been known for at Ruth's Chris. He also brought in chef George Panayiotou, son of famous Mobile restaurateur Constantine Panayiotou, who brought with him some classic Old Mobile recipes like turtle soup, Shrimp Constantine and sautéed softshell crab served on fried green tomatoes and his signature almondine sauce. The Cooper family of restaurants are known as some of the most popular of all of Mobile's restaurants.

Today, the Conde Cavaliers kick off the parading season in Mobile. Founded in 1977, the Condes, with their signature locomotive floats, always delight those in attendance. The Conde Cavaliers traditionally kick off parading in Mobile on the Friday night eighteen days before Fat Tuesday. At 6:30 p.m., the seventeen-float parade is lined up near the Mobile Civic Center, where most parades begin and end with a ball. Meanwhile, at the corner of Royal and St. Francis Streets, across from the Joe Cain Cafe, when the clock strikes a half past six o'clock, look to the sky for the fall of the Moon Pie while the sound of "Second Line" plays through the speakers surrounding the block. Restless kids await the sight of the first emblem float to round the corner. Men, women and children of all ages, races and socioeconomic backgrounds come together to enjoy Mardi Gras in Mobile. While this sense of revelry seems absurd to most people outside of the northern Gulf Coast, famous Mobilian and world traveler Eugene Walter sums up the celebration best: "If, as a child, you saw, every Mardi Gras, the figure of Folly chasing Death around the broken column of life, beating him on the back with a Fool's scepter…wouldn't you see the world in different terms, too?" Laissez les bon temps rouler!

11

HOME RUNS, HUDDLES AND HOMETOWN FAVORITES

A JOURNEY THROUGH MOBILE'S SPORTS HISTORY AT HEROES SPORTS BAR AND GRILLE

Mobile is a town that loves sports, with various sporting events happening throughout the year. Due to its average yearly temperature of seventy-six degrees, the town is an ideal location for outdoor sporting events. In January and February, while most places are preparing for winter, Mobile is getting ready for the annual Senior Bowl game. The Senior Bowl is an all-star game for senior college football players preparing to enter the NFL draft, and it has been held in Mobile since 1951. The event draws thousands of NFL personnel to the city for a week, including coaches, general managers, scouts, media and fans. Heroes Sports Bar and Grille, located on Dauphin Street in Mobile, is a popular spot for NFL personnel during Senior Bowl week. It has seen many famous NFL personalities over the years, such as John Elway, Jerry Rice, Pete Carroll, Bill Cowher and Jon Gruden.

David Rasp, the owner of Heroes Sports Bar and Grille, had no previous restaurant experience when he opened the establishment in November 1998. He opened the bar because his favorite sports bar, Big Kahuna's, closed down. Like many residents of Mobile, Rasp is a die-hard sports fan. Throughout the year, especially during college and pro football seasons, Heroes becomes a hub for sports fans, offering food and drink specials to celebrate the occasion. Other major sporting events are well celebrated at Heroes throughout the year such as the NCAA Basketball Tournament, Major League Baseball World Series, the Masters or even the US Open Tennis Championships.

A New Era of Eats

Heroes Sports Bar and Grille is a favorite among sports fans in Mobile. *Stacy Cole, 2019.*

Mobile has produced more Major League Baseball Hall of Famers than any other city outside of New York City and Los Angeles. Hank Aaron, Satchel Paige, Billy Williams, Willie McCovey and Ozzie Smith were all born in Mobile. These players, along with many others, make Mobile responsible for more home runs than any other city in the United States.

Although NFL and NCAA football are currently popular, Mobile has traditionally been a baseball town. While the origins of baseball in Mobile are not known, we do know its popularity was seen as early as the Civil War. The game of baseball can be traced back to Mobile as early as 1860 on the campus of Spring Hill College, six miles from downtown Mobile, when two brothers from Spring Hill, Nemisio Guillo and Enrique Porto Romaguera, brought a baseball and bat back home to Cuba during their summer break while attending the college. The sport had many different names and different rules at this time but eventually became known as baseball and America's pastime. In 1868, Nemisio founded the first baseball team in Cuba, called the Habana Base Ball Club. Over three hundred MLB Hall of Famers were born in Cuba, and their roots can be traced back to a game learned in Mobile, Alabama. The oldest continuously used baseball field in the United States is located at Spring Hill College and is called Stan Galle Field. The field dates to 1889, when it hosted its first game. The Badgers continue to play their home games at the stadium with the same historic backdrop as photos from the late nineteenth century.

Leroy Paige was born and raised in segregated Mobile. When Leroy was a boy growing up in Mobile, the local train station was a hub for wealthy White travelers going to and from the Port City. Meanwhile, Black workers engaged in manual labor such as shoveling coal into locomotives, and the young Black boys like Leroy worked as shoe shiners and baggage carriers for a $0.10 gratuitous wage. Leroy created a contraption that allowed him to carry up to four satchels at a time, earning him up to $0.40. His ingenuity caught the attention of the other boys, who laughed and nicknamed him "Satchel." The name stuck, and Satchel Paige went on to become a legendary baseball player in American history. Satchel was discovered in Mobile in the 1920s by a scout named Alex Herman from the Negro League Chattanooga White Sox. Herman found Paige throwing oyster shells at telegram poles on the streets of Mobile. Paige was signed to a $250/month Negro League contract with the Chattanooga White Sox, with $200 of his contract going to his mother to convince her that it was okay for her son to be away from home. Paige went on to become arguably the greatest pitcher in baseball history, with his powerful arm and deadly curveball.

Baseball was a popular sport among boys in Mobile during the 1940s and '50s. They played well into the night, using rags lit on fire to see the ball in the dark. Henry Aaron, one of the most famous baseball players of all time, grew up in the Toulminville community, just five miles from downtown Mobile. Henry and the boys from Toulminville played other communities like Whistler, where a young boy named Billy Williams was watching his older brother play. Billy was called on if they needed an extra player. At the same time, just a short bike ride across town in Magazine Point, a young man named Willie McCovey was the star of that field. All would go on to become MLB hall of famers but played baseball as youngsters growing up in Mobile. To be a good baseball player in Mobile really meant something in those days.

Henry Aaron, as he's known in Mobile, fondly recalls the moment that changed his life. He was a homesick boy. He was born and raised here and never left, so when he signed with the Boston Braves, he was scared to death to catch the train out of Mobile. As he was working his way up to the big leagues, Henry recalled a time he called home to say he was done, that he quit. He wanted to see his mother. His brother convinced him that their mama was fine and everything back home was fine, to keep playing and don't come back home. He said that moment changed his life; he kept working, made it to the big leagues and the rest is history for Henry Aaron. He went on to become an MLB hall of famer and the Home Run King

A New Era of Eats

Leroy "Satchel" Paige grew up in Mobile throwing oyster shells before he went on to throw baseballs. *Library of Congress.*

of baseball on April 8, 1974, when he nailed his 715th home run, breaking the record of Babe Ruth for most home runs in a career. Henry's impact was felt throughout the South but especially in his hometown. Cleon Jones was a young boy growing up in the Africatown community of Mobile, but when Aaron visited his school in 1954, that changed his life and he decided he wanted to become a professional baseball player. Cleon made it to the major leagues, as did Tommie Agee and Amos Otis, who all played for the 1969 New York Mets. The "Miracle Mets" won the World Series that year, defeating Henry Aaron and the Braves on the way to the title. Cleon Jones and Tommie Agee were starting outfielders for that championship team while Amos Otis came off the bench in relief. An outfield full of Mobilians. Something was certainly in the water in Mobile during that time. Henry Aaron, his brother Tommie Aaron, Willie McCovey, Billy Williams, Cleon Jones, Tommie Agee, Amos Otis and Jim Mason were all Mobilians playing Major League Baseball at the same time in the early 1970s.

The City of Mobile announced a minor-league franchise had been awarded to the city in the mid-1990s. The Mobile BayBears would compete in the Southern League as a AA-affiliate for the San Diego Padres. A stadium was built in 1997 and named after Mobile's native home run–hitting son. Hank Aaron Stadium opened to a sold-out crowd on its opening night on April 17, 1997, when Aaron himself threw out the very first pitch. The BayBears played their home games at "The Hank" in Mobile until the team left in 2019.

Mobile has attributed the impact of Henry Aaron all around the city. The Henry Aaron Loop surrounds the downtown corridor of Mobile along Water, Broad, and Canal Streets. Carver Park in Aaron's neighborhood of Toulminville was renamed Hank Aaron Park in honor of the boy who once played on those very grounds. Henry's childhood home was moved to the grounds of the stadium named in his honor. The Hank Aaron Childhood Home and Museum opened to the public in 2010. Many of the artifacts inside are a tribute to "Hammerin' Hank" and the rich history of baseball in Mobile.

Mobile's sports history is not limited to just baseball and football; the city also has a rich tradition in basketball, golf and tennis. Basketball has been played in Mobile since the early twentieth century, with the first high school teams forming in the 1920s. The boys' team from Barton Academy made it to the inaugural finals of the Alabama High School Athletic Association's

Henry Aaron cuts the ribbon on his childhood home that was relocated in 2010 to the stadium that bears his name, Hank Aaron Stadium. *Library of Congress.*

Basketball Tournament in 1921. One of Mobile's most famous basketball players is DeMarcus Cousins, who was born and raised in the city and graduated from LeFlore High School before going on to play college ball at Kentucky and star in the NBA. Jason Caffey was a graduate of Davidson High School in Mobile and went on to become the Gatorade Player of the Year in the state of Alabama. He played at the University of Alabama before becoming a first-round draft pick of the Chicago Bulls, where he starred with Michael Jordan on the great Bulls teams of the late 1990s. The University of South Alabama, located in Mobile, has a successful basketball program, and the Mitchell Center, the university's arena, is a popular venue for basketball games and other sporting events.

Golf is another sport with deep roots in Mobile, with the city boasting several top-quality courses, such as Azalea City Golf Course, Magnolia Grove Golf Course and Spring Hill College Golf Course. Magnolia Grove is a part of the Robert Trent Jones Golf Trail, which is a compilation of elite-level golf courses located throughout the state of Alabama. Magnolia Grove consistently ranks as one of the best golf courses in the United States to play.

Tennis is also popular in Mobile, with the Mobile Tennis Center being one of the largest public tennis facilities in the world. The center hosts numerous tournaments throughout the year, including the USTA Southern Sectional Championships and the USTA National Level 3 Junior Tournament. The Mobile Tennis Center is a testament to the city's commitment to providing world-class sporting facilities for both professional athletes and amateur enthusiasts.

Inside Heroes Sports Bar and Grille, visitors can experience a tribute to the famous athletes from the Mobile area, showcasing their impact on the sports world. The decor and memorabilia are carefully curated to provide a unique and inspiring atmosphere for sports fans and enthusiasts alike.

The food menu at Heroes is not to be missed, featuring a mouthwatering selection of sandwiches, burgers, wings and appetizers that are sure to satisfy any appetite. One of their signature sandwiches, the Clipper, is a delicious combination of smoked turkey breast, crispy bacon, sautéed mushrooms, Monterey jack cheese and a secret sauce, all served on grilled sourdough bread. For burger lovers, the Major League Melt is a must-try, featuring a juicy charbroiled patty topped with melted American cheese and sautéed onions, served on thick Texas toast. One of the most popular items on the menu is the spinach and crawfish dip, which takes the traditional spinach dip to the next level by adding crawfish and cream cheese, creating a unique and flavorful dish that is perfect for sharing. Throughout the year, you'll find specials like the red beans and rice, or if you're especially lucky, the kitchen will serve gumbo from their sister restaurant down the street, The Royal Scam. Whether you're a regular at Heroes, a first-time visitor or a hall of famer, the food is sure to impress.

During Senior Bowl week in early February, Heroes is especially busy, with visitors flocking to the restaurant to enjoy the delicious food and large beer selection. The restaurant is a popular spot for scouts and journalists covering the game, providing a relaxed atmosphere where they can unwind and connect with other members of the football community. For many, an evening at Heroes is a welcome break from the hectic schedule of the week, providing a space to socialize, share stories and create memories. It's no wonder that Heroes has become an institution and a staple of the Senior Bowl experience, eagerly anticipated by those in the football community year after year.

12

FROM REVITALIZATION TO REVOLUTION

THE CHEESE COTTAGE AND MOBILE'S TWENTY-FIRST-CENTURY FOOD SCENE

As the new millennium approached, Mobile underwent significant infrastructure developments in the late 1990s to reclaim its status as a thriving southern city. The banana docks were demolished to construct the Mobile Convention Center along the waterfront, attracting conferences and events. A state-of-the-art cruise terminal was built for Carnival Cruise Lines, transporting thousands of passengers to vacation destinations in Mexico and beyond.

In 2006, the RSA Tower, Alabama's tallest building, was completed. This development coincided with the renovation and reopening of the Battle House Hotel, a luxurious establishment that has since been awarded "Best Historic Hotel" by Historic Hotels of America. A strong workforce characterized Mobile's early twenty-first-century story, with Austal shipbuilding employing thousands to construct combat ships for the U.S. Navy. Airbus, operating its only North American facility, produced various aircraft models in Mobile. Steel mills along the Mobile River contributed to a constant stream of barges, trains and trucks transporting steel coils to automotive manufacturers and other industries.

Mobile's waterfront has always been the backbone of our economy, and that still rang true even after Mobile celebrated its tricentennial in 2002. Now with a robust shipbuilding industry and a thriving container shipping sector, Mobile has managed to secure its position as the ninth-busiest port in the United States. The city's flourishing shipbuilding industry caters to various sectors, including the U.S. Navy and commercial enterprises, and has generated numerous employment opportunities for the local population. Meanwhile, container shipping has enabled the seamless transportation of

The RSA Tower towers over the historic buildings in downtown Mobile. *Author's collection, 2023.*

goods both domestically and internationally, further bolstering Mobile's status as a vital trade hub. Ironically, container shipping was begun here in Mobile by Malcolm McClean, who owned a trucking company and later the Waterman Steamship Company. His idea was, instead of spending hours unloading trucks by crates onto the ships, a crane would pick up the trailer and place the entire container on the ship, saving thousands of hours of labor. The continued expansion of these industries has not only driven economic growth in Mobile but also played a crucial role in shaping the city's identity and future prospects.

The rise in popularity of fast food and fast-casual restaurants dominated the restaurant scene for the first decade of Mobile in the twenty-first century, but the second decade saw an explosion of growth in the downtown area that led to the establishment of over fifty locally owned restaurants. Dauphin Street had gone from boarded-up establishments to a thriving scene for food and drink lovers. Restaurants and bars line the two-mile stretch from Royal Street west to Washington Avenue. Even north of Dauphin Street to the once vacant St. Louis Street now has restaurants, breweries, bakeries and a grocery store. One of those restaurants located on St. Louis Street is The Cheese Cottage.

Kristi and Bubba Barber opened The Cheese Cottage in 2018 after Kristi's travels around the world with her corporate job. She frequently visited cheese shops in Europe and aspired to bring the culture of cheese board grazing and wine sipping to the Gulf Coast. Kristi stumbled upon an abandoned building on St. Louis Street that still retained some of its original historic character. This former Pure Oil gas station and service center, built in the 1920s, was designed to blend in with the neighborhood at that time. Bay windows and flower boxes surround the exterior, which features a steep roof and arched doorway that perfectly harmonized with the residential neighborhood. Pure Oil chose this design to differentiate themselves from their competitors, opting for a structure that blended in rather than a typical stand-alone filling station. After World War II, St. Louis Street boomed as "Automotive Alley," with car dealerships catering to returning veterans. However, in the 1970s, westward expansion in Mobile led these dealerships to move west along the newly built interstate, leaving St. Louis Street boarded up and abandoned. The building housing The Cheese Cottage had been deserted since 1980.

Now, The Cheese Cottage attracts locals and visitors from all over the country to St. Louis Street, offering dozens of different types of cheeses. Some are made from cow's milk, while others come from sheep's or goat's milk. Cheese is sourced from expected places like Wisconsin but also from Iowa and other dairies throughout the Southeast and even England, France and continental Europe. The menu changes every six months or with the seasons. Specials like their brunch, cheese-pairing classes or

The former Pure Oil filling station sat vacant for nearly forty years before becoming home to the Cheese Cottage in 2018. A testament to the revitalization found in downtown Mobile. *Author's collection, 2023.*

Raclette nights, which feature melted Swiss cheese served on potatoes, are very popular. Current owner Stephenie Funaro boasts a menu full of sandwiches, cheese boards, pizzas and a showcase container full of cheeses to take home for the perfect cheese board to impress guests you may be hosting.

Driving down St. Louis Street today reveals a renaissance of activity. The area has evolved into a high-tech corridor filled with local businesses, restaurants, breweries and more, reflecting the vibrant transformation and resurgence of Mobile's downtown and culinary scene.

Several entrepreneurs can be credited with the revitalization of Mobile's food scene, but one who started during Mobile's bleakest times was Chakli Diggs. A culinary visionary, Diggs has been delighting Mobilians with his creative cuisine since 1992. Opening his first restaurant, Bienville Bistro, on Conception Street, Chakli quickly became a pioneer in the city's food scene when not many others were willing to take those risks in the 1990s. In May 2005, Chakli opened NoJa, a fine dining establishment named after its location on North Jackson Street, just steps away from Dauphin Street.

The interior of the Cheese Cottage, a transformed building, once a Pure Oil filling station, nestled along the historic "Automotive Alley" on St. Louis Street. *Stacy Cole, 2019.*

With a vision similar to his first venture, Chakli wanted to bring a taste of Europe to downtown Mobile with NoJa. He focused on creating a sophisticated yet relaxed environment, highlighting the building's original architecture from the 1840s and providing a fresh alternative to the chain restaurants that dominated the food scene in Mobile at the time. NoJa's menu offers Mediterranean dishes with an Asian twist, reflecting Chakli's diverse international roots, which include his birthplace of Ethiopia, Germany, France and Texas. The menu changes seasonally, with weekly specials based on fresh regional ingredients.

NoJa's success is partly due to the passionate staff who have worked together for years, embracing Chakli's culinary philosophy. Chakli himself has an extraordinary background, having trained as a fighter pilot in Ethiopia before discovering his love for food and culture. He has traveled the world, gaining experience in various cuisines and languages, ultimately bringing his unique "MediterrAsian" fusion to Mobile. Chakli moved to Mobile from Germany, drawn by the city's fascinating downtown area and the evolving food scene. His dedication to excellence and perseverance has turned NoJa into a must-visit dining destination for residents and visitors alike.

Over the years, NoJa has welcomed notable patrons, including celebrities, prominent business owners and local politicians. Through his dedication to his craft, Chakli Diggs has left an indelible mark on Mobile's fine-dining culinary landscape, introducing unique flavor combinations and a new cultural cuisine that will be remembered and celebrated for years to come.

While a farm-to-table dining experience has long been part of Mobile's culinary history, the city, like many others across the country, started to see changing food trends beginning in the 1940s. During World War II, the U.S. Army, tasked with feeding millions of soldiers abroad, invested heavily in processed foods. This development, coupled with people moving away from farms and relying more on grocery stores for their food supply, gave rise to an entire generation of fast-food and processed food consumers. In response to this trend, the farm-to-table movement gained traction, and in 2013, Chef Chris Rainosek brought it to Mobile when he opened The Noble South.

The Noble South is a true farm-to-table restaurant using only local growers and farmers in the area while specializing in hydroponic greens and herbs. It's fresh ingredients with no pesticides or fertilizers in your food combined with the freshest ingredients of any restaurant in Mobile. The Noble South also helps support local farmers and harvesters. Popular menu items like the pickled shrimp come in a glass jar of seasoned pickles served with saltine crackers. At lunch, hungry patrons enjoy a variety of meats from catfish and pork chops to chicken thighs and meatloaf, served alongside black-eyed peas, greens, fried green tomato and beet salad. At dinner, wagyu brisket, pork belly and fresh redfish can be found on the menu. The Noble South has become a beloved destination for those seeking a genuine, farm-fresh dining experience in Mobile, located at 203 Dauphin Street overlooking historic Bienville Square.

Matt Lemond, a New Orleans transplant who chose to make the Port City his home after graduating from Spring Hill College, has arguably made one of the most significant impacts on Mobile's food and drink scene in the early twenty-first century. Upon his graduation, Matt wasted no time before diving into the bar industry, launching a small establishment on North Jackson Street. Soon after, he opened his second venture, O'Daly's Irish Pub, in 2009. The grand opening coincided with Super Bowl XLIV, a day made even more memorable as Matt's beloved New Orleans Saints triumphed over the Indianapolis Colts.

Situated in a part of Dauphin Street that had seen better days, O'Daly's was a testament to Matt's foresight. He saw potential in the wide-open field at the back of the location, which now hosts cornhole games, wiffleball tournaments and other events throughout the year, with St. Patrick's Day being their biggest annual celebration.

Over time, O Daly's evolved from a simple bar to a culinary destination with the addition of the adjacent Hole in the Wall kitchen. Serving up classic bar food like chicken wings and fried pickles, O'Daly's has become renowned for two signature dishes. One, the Trash Can Fries, are a decadent pile of fries topped with house-made roast beef, cheese curds and gravy. The other, the 504 Pizza, named after Matt's New Orleans area code, features blackened chicken, Conecuh sausage, mozzarella cheese and mushrooms, all finished with a Guinness glaze and a hint of hot sauce. This unique combination has quickly become one of the most sought-after pizza slices in Mobile.

In 2019, Matt ventured into a new niche with the opening of POST, an upscale wine bar situated just across the street from O'Daly's. While Matt likes to refer to POST as his "grown-up" bar, he is also a staunch advocate for men's mental health and has consciously designed the space to foster a sense of comfort and relaxation. Inspired by a visit to Ponce City Market in Atlanta and his subsequent travels, Matt was determined to introduce Mobile to the food hall concept. While shared dining spaces weren't new to Mobile, given the thriving food court that once graced Bel Air Mall in west Mobile, the trendy food hall concept was gaining popularity in revitalized urban areas throughout the country. Offering a range of food and drink vendors under one roof and furnished with communal seating and stylish decor, food halls were gaining traction. Entrepreneurs were drawn to the low start-up costs and high potential for success in well-marketed food halls.

With a suitable property on Dauphin Street, Matt seized the opportunity to bring his vision to life. In 2022, the Insider Food Hall opened its doors, treating customers to a culinary variety that included burgers, tacos, pizza, chicken and poke bowls. Next door is the Outsider Lounge, another venture run by Matt, who lets the food vendors focus on their craft while his team manages the bar, an area he's well-versed in. Further enhancing the locale's appeal, the Outsider is connected to another Lemond-owned property, the Cedar Street Social Club. This large event space, equipped with a stage for small band performances and events, works in harmony with Matt's other properties, offering food, drinks and entertainment to Mobilians all year.

POST, under the ownership of Matt Lemond in Mobile, Alabama, delights patrons with its exquisite food and wine offerings. *Author's collection, 2020.*

Undeniably, the most significant disruption to the restaurant industry in recent times has been the COVID-19 pandemic. On March 18, 2020, the Mobile County Health Department ordered the closure of all restaurants, bars and breweries for indoor dining for a week to encourage social distancing and curb the spread of the COVID-19 virus that was beginning to sweep the nation. What was initially intended as a one-week directive turned into a staggering seven-and-a-half-week shutdown in Mobile County. While some eateries were able to pivot to takeout or to-go services, others had no choice but to close their doors entirely. Among those affected was the newly inaugurated Mo'Bay Beignet Co.

Jaclyn Robinson, the creative force behind Mo'Bay Beignet Co., opened her beignet café in a historic 150-year-old building on Dauphin Street in the heart of downtown Mobile on February 6, 2020. Jaclyn's journey to owning her own café started when she began making beignets for her children on special occasions, later selling them at pop-ups and events as a fundraiser. Guided by her faith, she eventually decided to establish a permanent location at 451 Dauphin Street. In the first month following the grand opening, the café enjoyed an overwhelming reception, with long lines and hour-long wait times. Prior to the pandemic-enforced closure on March 18, Mo'Bay had sold an impressive total of over 100,000 beignets.

The secret to the popularity of Mo'Bay's beignets lies in their preparation. Each beignet is handcrafted from scratch upon each customer's order. However, the standout feature of Jaclyn's beignets, setting them apart from others along the Gulf Coast, is her homemade syrups. Made fresh daily in-house, the buttercream and cinnamon syrups are a treat. Moreover, a unique, rotating seasonal syrup is introduced each month. These range from strawberry in May and Grandma's Chocolate Gravy in January—named in honor of Jaclyn's grandmother—to a special Mardi Gras cream cheese during the Carnival season.

Despite the setback brought on by the pandemic, Mo'Bay Beignet Co. made a remarkable recovery and has since thrived. In the subsequent three years, the company expanded significantly, boasting over eight locations throughout the Southeast and six more within the state of Alabama.

Regrettably, not all restaurants emerged as triumphantly as Mo'Bay Beignet Co. from the upheaval caused by the COVID-19 pandemic. Numerous establishments had to permanently shut their doors, while others faced a sudden exodus of their furloughed staff who found employment elsewhere. This mass departure created a chasm in the hospitality workforce, putting immense pressure on many restaurateurs and driving some to abandon the industry altogether.

The year that followed the full reopening of dining rooms was marked by an intense demand for indoor dining. This surge of patrons, coupled with the intermittent closures necessitated when staff members fell ill,

Homemade syrups are the signature element on beignets from Mo'Bay Beignet Co. *Author's collection, 2022.*

bred chaos in an industry that is ordinarily known for its consistency. The once predictable rhythms of the restaurant business were upended, leaving many in the industry scrambling to adapt to these new and challenging circumstances. This abrupt change brought about an era of uncertainty and strain, reshaping the landscape of the restaurant industry in ways that continue to be felt.

The remarkable ascent of food tourism during the first two decades of the twenty-first century made a significant impact across the nation before it finally found its way to the Port City. The concept was introduced to Mobile in 2017 with the launch of the city's first food tour. Bienville Bites Food Tour uniquely offers guests a chance to savor an eclectic assortment of the finest culinary offerings in Mobile in a single, delightful experience.

Accompanied by friendly and knowledgeable tour guides, guests are led on a fascinating gastronomic journey, complete with an array of signature dishes that encapsulate the city's rich culinary heritage. This provides not only tourists but also locals with an unparalleled opportunity to explore and indulge in the vibrant food scene of Mobile.

Food tourism, beyond its obvious appeal to the palate, profoundly affects a city in various ways. It offers an authentic, sensory exploration of the local culture and history, as each dish tells a story about the region's heritage and traditions. It also significantly contributes to the local economy, generating revenue and creating jobs in the hospitality and tourism sectors.

Moreover, the success and popularity of food tours encourage innovation and diversity in the local culinary scene, as restaurants strive to offer unique and memorable dishes that appeal to both locals and tourists. This friendly competition fosters a dynamic and ever-evolving food culture that continually draws in new visitors while keeping locals excited and engaged.

Food tourism also plays a crucial role in boosting a city's international profile. As travelers share their culinary experiences on social media and review platforms, the reputation of the city's cuisine spreads globally, attracting more tourists and further enhancing the city's culinary prestige. The rise of food tourism in Mobile, embodied by initiatives like Bienville Bites Food Tour, has not only revolutionized the way locals and tourists experience the city's cuisine but also significantly contributed to the city's cultural vibrancy, economic growth and global recognition.

CONCLUSION

As we look toward the future, it's evident that Mobile's food scene is perfectly primed to make its mark on the global culinary stage throughout the remainder of the twenty-first century. With more than fifty restaurants nestled in the heart of downtown and numerous others scattered across city limits in neighborhoods like Oakleigh, Midtown, Dauphin Island Parkway (DIP), West Mobile and beyond, the sheer variety of culinary offerings reflects Mobile's rich and diverse gastronomic legacy.

Mobile's cuisine is not just about the food but a testament to over three centuries of history. Each dish, each ingredient and each cooking method carries with it the echoes of the past as well as the aspirations for the future. The city's culinary scene is intricately woven with threads of tradition, innovation, local produce and global influences, creating a vibrant and dynamic food scene that speaks to the heart and soul of Mobile.

What sets Mobile apart is the city's deep-rooted connection to its history and an unyielding commitment to local ingredients. Its food culture is a tribute to the region's rich heritage as a port city, the bounty of the Gulf of Mexico and the diverse cultures that have shaped its culinary identity. From the southern comfort food that draws on recipes passed down through generations to innovative fusion cuisine that pushes the boundaries of traditional cooking, Mobile's culinary landscape is as diverse as it is delicious.

At the heart of this culinary evolution are the city's dedicated chefs, restaurateurs and creators who continually strive to elevate Mobile's gastronomy to new heights. Their passion, creativity and commitment to preserving the city's culinary heritage while embracing new trends and techniques are key ingredients in Mobile's recipe for success on the world culinary stage.

As we step into the future, it is clear that Mobile's culinary legacy will continue to evolve, flourish and surprise. Its vibrant food scene is poised to delight locals and visitors alike with its unique blend of traditional flavors and innovative interpretations, further cementing its place as a world-class culinary destination. Indeed, the rich culinary history of Mobile is not just a testament to its past but a promising blueprint for a delicious future.

BIBLIOGRAPHY

Websites

Butch Cassidy's Café. https://butchcassidys.com.
Callaghan's Irish Social Club. https://callaghansirishsocialclub.com.
Cammie's Old Dutch Ice Cream Shoppe. https://cammiesolddutch.com.
Greek Fest Mobile. https://greekfestmobile.com.
Heroes Sports Bar & Grille. https://heroessportsbar.com.
Las Floriditas. https://lasfloriditas.com.
Mobile Mask. https://mobilemask.com.
The Noble South. https://noblesouthrestaurant.com.
The Royal Scam. https://royalscammobile.com.
Squid Ink. Eclectic Eats & Drinks. https://squidinkeats.com.
Three Georges. https://3georges.com.
United Fruit Company. https://unitedfruit.org/zemurray.htm.
Wintzell's Oyster House. https://wintzellsoysterhouse.com.

Interviews

Blohme, Pete. In-person interview. November 10, 2022.
Funaro, Stephenie. In-person interview. April 3, 2023.
Lemond, Matt. In-person interview. September 29, 2022.
Moore, George. In-person interview. February 7, 2023.

Patterson, Roosevelt. In-person interview. February 6, 2023.
Robinson, Jaclyn. In-person interview. October 4, 2022.

Books

Bergeron, Arthur, Jr. *Confederate Mobile.* Baton Rouge: Louisiana State University Press, 2000.
Bivens, Shawn A. *Mobile, Alabama's People of Color: A Tricentennial History, 1702–2002.* Vol. 1. Victoria, BC: Trafford Publishing, 2005.
Blejwas, Emily. *The Story of Alabama in Fourteen Foods.* Tuscaloosa: University of Alabama Press, 2019.
Bridges, Edwin C. *Alabama: The Making of an American State.* Tuscaloosa: University of Alabama Press, 2016.
Brueske, Paul. *The Last Siege: The Mobile Campaign, Alabama 1865.* Havertown, PA: Casemate, 2018.
Bunn, Mike. *Early Alabama: An Illustrated Guide to the Formative Years, 1798–1826.* Tuscaloosa: University of Alabama Press, 2019.
———. *Fourteenth Colony: The Forgotten Story of the Gulf South During America's Revolutionary Era.* Montgomery, AL: NewSouth Books, 2020.
Cohen, Rich. *The Fish That Ate the Whale: The Life and Times of America's Banana King.* New York: Picador, 2013.
Diouf, Sylviane A. *Dreams of Africa in Alabama.* Old Saybook, CT: Tantor Media Inc, 2019.
Door, Lisa Lindquist. *A Thousand Thirsty Beaches: Smuggling Alcohol from Cuba to the South During Prohibition.* Chapel Hill: University of North Carolina Press, 2018.
Edge, John T. *The New Encyclopedia of Southern Culture.* Vol. 7. Chapel Hill: University of North Carolina Press, 2014.
Hurston, Zora Neale. *Barracoon: The Story of the Last "Black Cargo."* New York: Amistad Press, 2018.
Raines, Ben. *The Last Slave Ship: The True Story of How Clotilda Was Found, Her Descendants, and an Extraordinary Reckoning.* New York: Simon & Schuster, 2022.
Roberts, L Craig. *Mardi Gras in Mobile.* Charleston, SC: Arcadia Publishing, 2015.
Sledge, John. *The Gulf of Mexico: A Maritime History.* Columbia: University of South Carolina Press, 2019.
———. *The Mobile River.* Columbia: University of South Carolina Press, 2015.

Steiner, Malcolm. *Old Mobile Restaurants*. Mobile, AL: M. Steiner, 2009.
Thomason, Michael. *Historic Mobile: An Illustrated History of the Mobile Bay Region*. San Antonio, TX: Historical Publishing Network, 2010.
Waselkov, Greg. *Old Mobile Archaeology*. Tuscaloosa: University of Alabama Press, 2005.

Online Sources

Alsen, Dana. "The Alabama Food Frontier: Development of a Cuisine, 800 to the Present." Southern Foodways Alliance. https://alabamafoodways.org/.
Bellingrath Gardens and Home. "History." https://bellingrath.org.
Canadian Museum of History. "Virtual Museum of New France." https://www.historymuseum.ca.
Dumas, Michael. "Kazoola Brings Unity to Mobile through Food and Music." AL.com, December 6, 2019. https://www.al.com.
Edge, John T. "Dropping Inn at a Mobile Institution." *Garden and Gun*, August/September 2021. https://gardenandgun.com.
Gentry, Jill Clair. "The Resurgence of Automobile Alley." *Mobile Bay*, December 20, 2018. https://mobilebaymag.com.
Holloway, David. "'Messlords' and Their Brand of Zany, Culinary Magic to Benefit Alabama Veterans." AL.com, February 11, 2013. https://www.al.com.
Irwin, Ned L. "Morrison's Cafeteria." *Encyclopedia of Alabama*. https://encyclopediaofalabama.org.
Lacey, Maggie. "Restaurant Review: Kazoola Eatery & Entertainment." *Mobile Bay*, August 30, 2017. https://mobilebaymag.com.
Maisel, Ivan. "Mobile's Landmark Goober Shop." *Garden and Gun*, August/September 2022. https://gardenandgun.com.
Massouleh McCay, Tara. "The Oldest Restaurant in Mobile, Alabama, Is Credited with Introducing the City to Hot Dogs." *Southern Living*, September 8, 2022. https://www.southernliving.com.
Matthews, Michelle. "How West Indies Salad Became an Iconic Alabama Dish." AL.com, September 16, 2018. https://www.al.com.
McGehee, Tom. "Ask McGehee: What Is the History of the Vacant Van Antwerp Building?" *Mobile Bay*, May 27, 2013. https://mobilebaymag.com.
———. "Ask McGehee: What Is the Story Behind Morrison's Cafeteria Chain?" *Mobile Bay*, April 6, 2020. https://mobilebaymag.com.

———. "The Gardens That Coke Built: Mr. Bell's Mobile Franchise." Bellingrath Gardens & Home. https://bellingrath.org.
Muskat, Carrie. "Billy Williams Shares Fond Memories of McCovey." Major League Baseball, November 1, 2018. https://www.mlb.com.
Prickett, Sam. "America's Oldest Continuously Operating Baseball Diamond Is in Alabama." This Is Alabama, June 23, 2021. https://www.thisisalabama.org.
Rhodes, Jesse. "The Legumes of War: How Peanuts Fed the Confederacy." *Smithsonian Magazine*, April 19, 2012. https://www.smithsonianmag.com.
Saucier Family Geneaology. "The Pelican Girls." https://thesaucierfamily.weebly.com.
Schrubbe, Georgia. "Our Cuban Connection." *Mobile Bay*, May 27, 2013. https://mobilebaymag.com.
Shestakofsky, Jon. "Loveable Cub: Billy Williams Parlayed a Textbook Swing and Unwavering Consistency into a Plaque in Cooperstown." National Baseball Hall of Fame, https://baseballhall.org.
Specker, Lawrence. "Mike Epps Takes a Walk on Dauphin Street, Shows Fans 'My New Band.'" AL.com, March 19, 2015. https://www.al.com.
———. "Restaurants We Miss in Mobile." AL.com, April 8, 2021. https://www.al.com.
———. "Squid Ink Happens: Downtown Mobile Gets New Flavors." AL.com, August 5, 2019. https://www.al.com.
Stephens, Regan. "This Old Gas Station in Mobile, Alabama, Is the Cheese Shop of Our Dreams." *Food & Wine*, June 15, 2022. https://www.foodandwine.com.
Thibodeaux, Ron. "Antoine de la Mothe, Sieur de Cadillac." 64 Parishes. https://64parishes.org.
Thomason, Michael. "Mobile Spirits." *Mobile Bay*, May 16, 2012. https://mobilebaymag.com.
———. "What's In a Nickname?" *Mobile Bay*, https://mobilebaymag.com.
Thorn, John. "Cuba, the U.S., and Baseball: A Long If Interrupted Romance." *Our Game*, March 21, 2016. https://ourgame.mlblogs.com.
Thurm, Wendy. "Mobile, Alabama: Birthplace of Hall of Famers." SBNation, July 22, 2012. https://www.sbnation.com.
United Fruit Company. "Samuel Zemurray 1877–1961." United Fruit Historical Society, https://www.unitedfruit.org/zemurray.htm.

Exhibits

Blackwell, Cart. *From Chicken on a Stick to Fancy Fare: Carnival and Cuisine.* January 8, 2022–April 30, 2022, Mobile Carnival Museum, Mobile, AL.

McCrummen-Fowler, Meg. *A History of Mobile in 22 Objects.* October 30, 2020–September 21, 2023, History Museum of Mobile, Mobile, AL.

Historical Markers

Dora Finley Franklin African American Heritage Trail of Mobile, 2020. The UNESCO Slave Route: Resistance, Liberty, Heritage. Mobile, Alabama

ABOUT THE AUTHOR

Chris Andrews is the founder and CEO of Bienville Bites Food Tour in Mobile, Alabama, and Taste of Fairhope in Fairhope, Alabama. He's also the host of the *Port City Plate* podcast, a biweekly exploration of the city's vibrant culinary scene. Born in Mobile and a graduate of Satsuma High School, Chris combined his passion for food and history in 2017 when he launched the first and only food tour in Mobile.

Since then, Bienville Bites has been named the "Best Food Tour in Alabama" and has consistently received the "Certificate of Excellence" by TripAdvisor, an award given to the top 10 percent of attractions worldwide based on excellent five-star reviews. In 2023, the tour was nominated as one of USA Today's 10 Best Food Tours in the country.

In the fall of 2020, Chris and his wife, Laney, launched the Taste of Fairhope tour, giving people an opportunity to connect through food and drink on both sides of Mobile Bay. His work in the podcast and food tours demonstrates Chris's passion for connecting people to the city through food and drink while giving them experiences and stories to share with others.

About the Author

When not sampling the city's best eats or engaging with listeners on his podcast, Chris enjoys spending time with his wife, Laney, and three children, Audrey, Sawyer and Carson. This is his first published book.

Visit us at
www.historypress.com